MAIN LINES
TO THE WEST

MAIN LINES
TO THE WEST

Simon Rocksborough-Smith

LONDON

IAN ALLAN LTD

First published 1981

ISBN 0 7110 1117 6

Published by Ian Allan Ltd, Shepperton, Surrey;
and printed by Ian Allan Printing Ltd at their works
at Coombelands in Runnymede, England

Contents

Preface and Acknowledgements

It started as an account of the Waterloo to Exeter line and its branches from about 1948 to the present day. I have known the line fairly well, but there were parts I wanted to learn more about; and now I only wish, for instance, that I had spent a few hours at Axminster or Seaton Junction on a Saturday in August 1958. Then I set to work on the line from Paddington, via the Berks & Hants route, Castle Cary and Taunton. It became rather depressing to chronicle the closure of branch lines and country stations (some not so small) in the 1960s, and the present day had repeatedly to be brought up to date, so I decided to write about my favourite period, the 1950s and (on the Southern, where changes came more slowly) the early 1960s. The details have been gleaned from timetables and working documents of the period, magazines, unofficial traffic surveys, from my own notebooks, and not least from the recollections of others. I am particularly grateful to Peter Tunks for letting me make use of his exhaustive knowledge of train working in the Honiton area; also to Ronald A. Lumber, Michael Hedges, Ian J. Turnbull, Roger Whitehouse and Mark B. Warburton, all of whom have helped me with personal observations or other information. For the Portrait of 1953 I have to thank J. N. Faulkner, John R. Fairman, Michael Hedges and Peter Tunks for the lengthy and absorbing notes they sent me about Saturday 8 August, and David St John Thomas for his counts of passenger loadings.

The majority of the photographs are from the Ian Allan Library, and I thank all those who have indirectly provided them. But I am especially indebted to R. C. Riley and Ronald A. Lumber, who allowed me to visit their homes and select a quantity of pictures, and who have spent time looking up obscure details about the pictures they took; also to Kenneth Leech and Ian J. Turnbull for the use of prints from their personal collections. Every picture, I think, illustrates some aspect of the book, although, because of timetable changes over the years, some of the trains shown are not exactly as described in the text.

Finally I would like to thank Michael Harris, editor of *Railway World* for his encouragement and many useful ideas.

Simon Rocksborough Smith
Wimbledon
November 1979

PART ONE

Waterloo to Exeter

Inter-city expresses from Bournemouth to Waterloo have to climb on to a flyover at Battledown to cross another line sweeping in from the west. There is less need for a flyover now than when it was built over 80 years ago; but this was the London & South Western main line to Exeter, the route of Drummond's express engines, the boat specials racing up from Plymouth, the 'King Arthurs' between the wars, the 'Atlantic Coast Express' and the Bulleid Pacifics.

In its heyday even the stretch from Waterloo to Basingstoke was known as the West of England main line, although shared with the line to Bournemouth and Weymouth. From Worting junction, west of Basingstoke and near Battledown flyover, it was a double-track express line, almost free of major speed restrictions. Further west it cut across a series of valleys, and became increasingly hilly, culminating in the climb to Honiton tunnel. There were no water troughs, and steam expresses between Exeter and Waterloo had to stop en route to take water or change engines. The usual place was Salisbury, but the Plymouth boat trains changed engines at Templecombe and passed Salisbury nonstop until the disastrous derailment at Salisbury curve in 1906.

The railway first reached Salisbury in 1847, when a branch was constructed from the London & Southampton main line at Bishopstoke, now Eastleigh. It terminated at Milford, which subsequently became an important goods station. Between 1854 and 1857 the direct line from Worting was opened, and later reached the site of the present Salisbury station through Bishopdown tunnel. In 1859 and 1860 the whole line from Salisbury to Exeter was completed, terminating at Exeter Queen Street, now Central.

A connecting line was laid in 1862 from Queen Street to the Bristol & Exeter Railway at St Davids, and in the same year the London & South Western Railway gained control of a broad gauge line which then extended the other side of Exeter as far as Bideford. A narrow-gauge rail was soon added, and to this move the expresses which ran until the 1960s from Waterloo to the Atlantic coast and Plymouth owed their existence.

In the 1950s and early 1960s there was nothing unusual in Bulleid Pacifics reaching 80mph and over on the downhill stretches, 85mph being the overall speed limit (except in the London suburbs). Leaving Waterloo, the railway climbs gradually through south-west London and Surrey to the 31st mile post. Beyond Woking, junction for Portsmouth, it crosses miles of heathland, much of it covered by the military camps of Aldershot and Farnborough, and finally emerges into open country after Fleet. West of Basingstoke the line becomes gradually more undulating, and after Andover crosses the edge of Salisbury Plain. The highest point on this section is near Grateley, followed by a quick descent through Porton into Salisbury. From there the line follows the course of the River Nadder up towards Semley, then leaves Wiltshire and keeps close to the Dorset-Somerset border for many miles, down to the River Stour at Gillingham, up to Buckhorn Weston tunnel, and down across the Blackmore Vale before Templecombe. After several more ups and downs the line falls continuously for 13 miles from Hewish, near Crewkerne, along the River Axe and into Devonshire. Leaving the Axe before Seaton Junction, westbound trains face Honiton bank, the steepest climb between Waterloo and Exeter, with five miles at 1 in 80. Beyond Honiton tunnel two more valleys are crossed, the Otter, near Sidmouth Junction (now Feniton) and the Clyst, before the final descent into Exeter.

During the 1950s there was a service of express trains about every two hours, leaving Waterloo on the hour and Exeter Central mainly on the half-hour. Most had through portions for Plymouth Friary, Ilfracombe and Torrington, and restaurant and tavern cars as far as Exeter Central.

Express engines were no longer changed at Salisbury as a regular practice after 1950. 'Merchant Navy' class engines, which were not permitted beyond Exeter because of their weight, were generally provided between Waterloo and Exeter Central when available, although 'West Country' and 'Battle of Britain' light Pacifics were often used. All the regular London trains changed engines at Exeter Central.

The tavern cars were a notable feature of those West of England expresses at this period. There were eight in all,

introduced in 1949 to a design by Bulleid. In the 1950s they were generally all operating on the Southern Region, mostly on the West of England line. They ran paired with an ordinary dining car, and consisted of a kitchen at one end, and at the other a bar designed like a public house in imitation timber. Each had a name, such as *The Salutation* or *The Jolly Tar*, which was carried on a pictorial sign painted on the outside. They were not very popular, partly because you could scarcely see out whilst eating, and towards the end of the 1950s they were converted to standard buffet cars.

Above: *By the time a westbound train reaches Honiton station it is descending quite steeply towards Sidmouth Junction. Class S15 No 30823 passes on a down freight on 21 July 1958.* R. C. Riley

List of Tavern Cars

	Number	Name	Regular duty summer 1955 Monday to Thursday
(A)	7892	*The White Horse*	12.18 Exeter Central-Waterloo (1st part ACE) when running
	7893	*The Jolly Tar*	13.00 Waterloo-Exeter Central
			17.55 Exeter Central-Waterloo
	7894	*The Dolphin*	11.05 Bournemouth West-Waterloo
			18.30 Waterloo-Bournemouth West
	7895	*The Bull*	12.30 Exeter Central-Waterloo (ACE)
			17.00 Waterloo-Exeter Central next day (staffed to Yeovil Junction)
	7896	*The Salutation*	'The Royal Wessex': Bournemouth West-Waterloo return
	7897	*The Three Plovers*	11.00 Waterloo-Exeter Central (ACE)
			16.30 Exeter Central-Waterloo
(A)	7898	*The Green Man*	11.05 Waterloo-Exeter Central (relief ACE) when running
	7899	*The George & Dragon*	10.30 Exeter Central-Waterloo
			18.00 Waterloo-Exeter Central

Each tavern car ran paired with a composite restaurant saloon (Nos 7833-7840).
(A) — alternate day working

The most celebrated train on this route was undoubtedly the 'Atlantic Coast Express'. The name was given in the summer of 1926, although there had for many years been a mid-morning express from Waterloo to the West, and it ran for the last time in September 1964. In the 1950s the down train for most of the year had nine separate portions, although the basic winter load was only 11 coaches. The portions were for Ilfracombe, Torrington, Padstow, Bude, Plymouth Friary, Exeter Central, Exmouth, Sidmouth, Seaton. At the height of the summer the up and down trains ran in two sections, dividing the various through coaches between them, but for most of the 1950s the summer relief train was advertised only in the up direction. The through coaches for Ilfracombe, Torrington, Padstow and Bude were, rightly, the only ones strictly designated 'Atlantic Coast Express'; they carried the name on roofboards but the rest of the train did not.

The 'Atlantic Coast Express', or 'ACE', made its first stop at Salisbury, where, if no relief was running, the Seaton coach was detached and joined to a Salisbury to Exeter stopping train which conveyed it as far as Seaton Junction. The main train's next stop was Sidmouth Junction, where the Exmouth and Sidmouth coaches were removed, then Exeter Central, where the restaurant and tavern cars came off and the remainder of the train was divided in two. In the up direction the same stops were made, but there were no portions from Exmouth, Sidmouth or Seaton; instead through coaches were attached at Salisbury from Yeovil Town and, in summer, Lyme Regis. These were conveyed to Salisbury by a stopping train originating at Ilfracombe.

Booked Formation of Down ACE

Summer 1954 (early and late season midweek)

Padstow	2 brake composites
Bude	1 brake composite
Plymouth	2 set: brake third saloon, brake composite
Ilfracombe	1 third, 1 brake composite
Torrington	1 brake composite
Exeter Central	1 tavern car, 1 refreshment saloon
Exmouth	1 brake composite
Sidmouth	1 brake composite
Seaton	1 brake composite

Winter 1963

Ilfracombe	3 set: brake second, composite, brake second
Padstow	3 set (as Ilfracombe), 2 seconds
Exeter Central	1 kitchen buffet car, 1 restaurant composite open, 1 brake composite

All coaches side corridor with compartments unless otherwise stated.

In 1952 the 'ACE' was accelerated to run faster than its prewar schedule, and for many years thereafter the down train's timing of 83min from Waterloo to Salisbury was the only mile-a-minute run on the Southern Region. It was easily the fastest train of the day between Waterloo and Exeter; for most of the 1950s the down train left London at 11.00 and reached Exeter Central at 14.05, and the up train left Exeter Central at 12.30 and terminated at 15.40. With the next acceleration in 1961 the Waterloo to Exeter timing was cut to less than 3hr in each direction, and at that period the Western Region, with diesel power, had only three trains, in either direction, with a faster timing between London and Exeter.

The other named train was perhaps more spectacular but less successful. In June 1947 the Southern Railway introduced the all-Pullman 'Devon Belle' between Waterloo and Ilfracombe and Plymouth, one reason being that after the war the Southern had a surplus of Pullman cars but a shortage of ordinary stock. The 'Devon Belle' left both Waterloo and Ilfracombe at 12.00 and ran from Friday to Monday only. There were two train sets, each with an observation car at the back, converted from an ordinary Pullman coach. The observation car ran to Ilfracombe, and at the end of the journey had to be turned on the turntable there; this was also at one time the only function of the Waterloo station turntable. The train divided at Exeter Central, the Ilfracombe portion being formed at the rear in each direction.

The 'Devon Belle' ran for eight summer seasons before being withdrawn. It had no advertised stop between Waterloo and Sidmouth Junction, but in fact changed engines at Wilton South, the next station west of Salisbury. For reasons mainly of prestige, Salisbury was passed without stopping; this had been prohibited since the accident of 1906, but was allowed for the 'Devon Belle' at a maximum speed of 10mph. A 'Merchant Navy' generally made the return journey between Waterloo and Wilton, where a fresh engine would be waiting in a bay with the headboard already in position.

After 1949 the through coaches to Plymouth Friary were withdrawn, and what had been the Plymouth portion ran between Waterloo and Exeter Central only. From 1948 there was an additional weekly journey in each direction, down on Thursday and up on Tuesday, but in 1952 the service began to contract; during the final season in 1954 a Friday evening departure from Waterloo was tried at 16.40. After withdrawal the observation cars appeared from time to time on excursions and land cruises, and one now belongs to the Dart Valley Railway; some of the ordinary Pullman cars were sent to the Western Region to form the new 'South Wales Pullman'.

The remaining Waterloo expresses made a number of stops before Exeter Central. There was one nonstop run in each direction between Yeovil Junction and Exeter and one between Templecombe and Sidmouth Junction, distances of just under 50 miles. The next fastest up train after the 'Atlantic Coast Express' was the first of the day leaving Exeter Central at 07.30 with almost a mile-a-minute booking from Andover Junction to Waterloo. In

Above: *In the early 1950s 'West Country' No 34037* Clovelly *climbs Honiton bank with an express from Portsmouth to Plymouth. This must be either the Sunday version of the 11.30 Brighton, which started from Portsmouth & Southsea at 11.40, or, if a Saturday in summer, the 09.03 Portsmouth & Southsea to Salisbury extended to Plymouth.* F. R. Hebron

Below: *Towards the end of steam the Bulleid Pacifics were not always fully extended by their duties. 'Battle of Britain' No 34056* Croydon *is near Milborne Port on Saturday 15 August 1964 with the 17.05 Yeovil Junction to Templecombe stopping train.* R. C. Riley

1957 an earlier train at 06.30 from Exeter was introduced, which took exactly the same time to Waterloo as the 07.30 but with different stops; this replaced the semi-fast 06.55 Yeovil Town to Waterloo, but the coaches of the Yeovil train were added to the back of the Exeter train at Salisbury, providing a through service to Waterloo. In the down direction the closest rival to the 'ACE' for speed was the 19.00 Waterloo to Plymouth, also introduced in 1957 with Salisbury its first stop.

The time honoured through Brighton to Plymouth train of course ran during the 1950s, with restaurant or buffet car for the whole distance, and coaches from Portsmouth & Southsea attached at Fareham. The journey was normally shared between two engines, a Brighton 'West Country' officially, but numerous other classes were used as well, as far as Salisbury, and an Exmouth Junction or Plymouth light Pacific for the rest of the way, no change being made at Exeter.

The through coaches from Exmouth and Sidmouth to Waterloo were conveyed from Sidmouth Junction by the 08.15 from Plymouth Friary (10.30 Exeter Central). At Templecombe the same train attached a through coach from Seaton which had been picked up by an Exeter to Templecombe stopping train. In the down direction both the 13.00 and 15.00 Waterloo to Plymouth detached coaches at Templecombe which worked forward as stopping trains to Exeter Central, and in the case of the 13.00 included a through coach for Lyme Regis in the summer.

Above: *In the early 1950s up to five different diesels were at work on the Southern Region (Western Section). Here No 10202 leaves Platform 10 at Waterloo in December 1951 with the 13.00 to Plymouth.* B. A. Butt

Most of the express engine diagrams were handled by Nine Elms and Exmouth Junction sheds, both of which had a stud of 'Merchant Navies' as well as light Pacifics. Salisbury also had three 'Merchant Navies' and a number of 'Battle of Britain' Pacifics. In the early 1950s up to five prototype diesels were working on the Southern main lines, Nos 10001/2 of the London Midland Region and Nos 10201/2/3 of the Southern Region. Between the end of 1951 and 1954 diesel locomotives frequently worked a turn involving two round trips from Waterloo to Exeter Central in 24 hours, starting at 01.25 and finishing at 22.08. Another diesel turn included reaching Waterloo at 10.00 from Bournemouth and leaving again an hour later with the down 'Atlantic Coast Express' as far as Exeter.

A number of 'King Arthurs' were shedded at Salisbury, and by the 1950s were mainly used on stopping passenger and freight trains, although they were occasionally given express passenger duties. Most freight traffic was in the hands of the 'S15' 4-6-0s, and the mixed traffic 'H15s' appeared on stopping passenger, parcels and freight trains. Moguls of Classes U and N were also used on local trains.

Above: *A typical freight train of the Southern Region's West of England main line passes Sherborne in the up direction on 31 July 1950 behind Class S15 No 30830.*   P. H. Wells

Below: *Class S15 No 30826 climbs from Seaton Junction to Honiton tunnel with the 15.34 Templecombe to Exeter Central stopping train, a milk tank bringing up the rear. The train includes through coaches off the 13.00 Waterloo to Plymouth, detached at Templecombe.*   J. C. Beckett

Locomotive Allocations — July 1953

Class	Salisbury 72B	Yeovil 72C	Exmouth Jct 72A
'Merchant Navy' 4-6-2	4		8
'West Country' 4-6-2			23
'Battle of Britain' 4-6-2	7		7
'King Arthur' 4-6-0	7		
H15 4-6-0	6		
S15 4-6-0	12		5
U 2-6-0	3	8	
N 2-6-0			18
T9 4-4-0	4	2	
700 0-6-0	4		
0395 0-6-0			3
Z 0-8-0T	1		1
BR 3MT 2-6-2T			6
Ivatt 2MT 2-6-2T			2
E4 0-6-2T	2		
E1/R 0-6-2T			4
0415 4-4-2T			3
M7 0-4-4T	2	1	17
O2 0-4-4T		1	4

Double heading of the heavier engines was not permitted on the Exeter main line except west of Seaton Junction. On this stretch it was sometimes necessary on summer Saturdays when the engine of a through Waterloo to Seaton train had to be worked to Exmouth Junction shed.

In the 1950s the West of England main line had an irregular but generous service of stopping trains along its length. Between Salisbury and Exeter Central, exclusive, there were 19 passenger stations, compared with nine in the 1970s, and as an example six down and five up trains

called each weekday at the hamlet of Sutton Bingham, while Semley had 10 or 11 trains in each direction. Main line stopping trains generally consisted of three or more corridor coaches and often some vans, and began or ended their journeys principally at Salisbury, Templecombe or Yeovil Town. Some ran through to or from Ilfracombe or Plymouth, and there were many starting at Exeter Central for points west, since Southern trains did not use Exeter St Davids as a terminus. Some stopping trains between Salisbury or Templecombe and Exeter changed engines at Yeovil Junction, for example the lunchtime Salisbury to Exeter stopper in each direction. East of Salisbury a number were through Waterloo trains, mostly running nonstop between Waterloo and Woking.

All the stations on the line were open for freight in the 1950s, and had their daily pick-up goods trains. Among the main through freight traffic were milk, cattle, ballast from Meldon and cider from Whiteways at Whimple. Meldon Quarry, near Okehampton, supplied railway ballast to all three divisions of the Southern Region, and there were paths for through trains to the depots at Woking, Three Bridges, New Cross Gate and Tonbridge. An express newspaper train, conveying passengers, left

Below: *On 5 September 1964, the penultimate day of through Southern expresses between Waterloo and places west of Exeter, No 34079* 141 Squadron *on the 08.25 Plymouth to Waterloo appears to have needed assistance and was piloted by No 34106* Lydford. *The picture shows the train coasting down the bank towards Templecombe (the prohibition against double-heading east of Seaton Junction did not apply to Light Pacifics). As it happened, the author saw this train passing Surbiton, by which stage the pilot had been removed and No 34079 was continuing single handed.* John H. Bird

Above: *The Sunday 18.30 Salisbury to Templecombe local was in fact the Clapham Junction to Exeter milk empties conveying one brake composite coach. Here the train, hauled by No 34002* Salisbury, *approaches Semley, where it was booked to shunt milk tanks for eight minutes, on 17 May 1964. This coach (usually two in summer) in fact made the whole journey, although it was empty except between Salisbury and Templecombe, and it returned to London on Monday's 'Atlantic Coast Express'.* W. G. Sumner

Below: *'Schools' class 4-4-0 No 30916* Whitgift, *recently transferred to Nine Elms, arrives at Yeovil Junction on duty 23 on 10 July 1959. The duty involved leaving Waterloo for Salisbury at 07.20, then hauling the 12.46 Salisbury to Exeter Central slow as far as Yeovil Junction. On this occasion the 12.46, which included a through coach off the 11.05 Waterloo to Padstow, was taken forward by No 34038* Lynton, *while No 30916 was turned on the Yeovil Junction turntable and then ran light to Yeovil shed.* R. C. Riley

Above: *The banker spur (foreground) is empty, but 'Battle of Britain' No 34053* Sir Keith Park *will no doubt wait for assistance up to Exeter Central with its train of ballast from Meldon Quarry, seen approaching St Davids on 27 June 1952.* W. S. Garth

Below: *No 34035* Shaftesbury *takes the down West of England line at Battledown with the 15.54 Clapham Junction to Exmouth Junction milk empties in April 1949. The down Bournemouth line is on the extreme right and the up Bournemouth line is out of sight to the left on an embankment.* M. W. Earley

Waterloo every night for Ilfracombe, Bideford, Plymouth and Padstow.

There were regular express freights at night between Nine Elms and the West of England, some of which were diagrammed for 'Merchant Navy' Pacifics east of Exeter. A train of empty milk tanks, usually Pacific-hauled, left Clapham Junction at 15.54 for stations to Exeter. Full tanks left the country stations in the early evening by several trains for the London area; in the early 1950s there was a daily through milk train from Yeovil to Gravesend. Some milk trains conveyed passengers for part of their journeys, such as Yeovil Junction to Semley, but there were often long waits at stations while tanks were marshalled.

All trains on the main line, passenger and freight, carried the headcode for Waterloo or Nine Elms and Plymouth, a white disc below the chimney and another in the centre of the buffer beam. On one of the discs was often shown the engine duty number, batches of which were assigned to the various sheds. These were altered from time to time, but West of England expresses worked by Nine Elms engines generally had duty numbers between 1 and 20, while a number in the middle 400s generally denoted Salisbury, and the late 400s and early 500s Exmouth Junction. Extra trains were normally handled by engines on special duties, and carried a number with the letters SPL in front.

Below: *Class H15 No 30332 arrives at Waterloo with a semi-fast train from Salisbury in August 1951.* P. Ransome-Wallis

Stations and Junctions

Waterloo to Worting junction

The first $50\frac{1}{4}$ miles are of a different character to the rest, with four tracks throughout, and other important flows of traffic, and so it is only proposed to refer to those features which affected the West of England trains.

Waterloo station, with its 21 platforms, is divided for operating purposes into three sections, Suburban, Main and Windsor, and these are controlled by separate panels in the signalbox. Except in the case of electric and semi-fast steam trains, the coaches of arriving trains were not normally (other than at holiday times) turned round in the platforms to form departures, as nowadays, but were taken out empty to be cleaned and serviced, and likewise the coaches for departing trains were brought in empty.

Thus important trains for the Exeter line generally left from Platform 9 or 10 (the only ones with their own bookstall), and arrived at Platform 13 or 14, while the

Below: *A line-up of evening departures at Waterloo on Wednesday 29 August 1962. From left to right: No 34018* Axminster *heads the 17.30 to Bournemouth West in Platform 11; No 34030* Watersmeet *the 17.23 'Holland American' Southampton Docks boat train for* ss Rotterdam *in Platform 10; and No 73110 the 17.43 to Salisbury (Platform 9). Just visible in Platform 4 is the 17.27 electric train to Portsmouth & Southsea (headcode 57). The 17.23, being a special working, has duty No SPL 6.* Ian J. Turnbull

Basingstoke and Salisbury semi-fasts used Platforms 7 and 8 for the most part.

The maximum length of train allowed into Waterloo was 13 coaches (a rule rarely broken), and only three of the platforms could take even this number, allowing for the engine. Empty trains which were up to the maximum length for the platform had to be brought in by a tank engine, and as likely as not the train engine would be standing ahead of the starting signal and fouling the track circuit, and would have to be signalled out by hand signal with a yellow or green flag.

The running lines out of Waterloo were then called through or local (as those on the Brighton line still are), instead of fast or slow. An express departing from Platform 9, 10 or 11 naturally took the down through line, signified by the letters MT on the indicator next to the starting signal (M for Main as opposed to Windsor), while in the up direction the through line branched into two at Vauxhall, the main through and main relief, and a train bound for Platform 13 or 14 more often approached on the up main relief.

The principal carriage depot and sidings for steam trains were at Clapham Yard (no part of which was electrified in the 1950s) in the fork between the diverging main and Windsor lines at Clapham Junction. Empty trains between Clapham and Waterloo were handled mostly by a large stud of 'M7' tank engines allocated to Nine Elms shed, or sometimes by one of the Class E4 carriage pilots, a large 'H16' goods tank, or by a main line engine on its (indirect) way between the terminus and shed. There were no independent carriage lines into or out of Waterloo, and on a normal day an up empty stock train would take the through line immediately east of Clapham Junction, and so have to be timed to fit in with all the fast steam and electric trains making for Waterloo. In the other direction, after a steam train had arrived, at whatever platform, its stock would almost invariably leave for Clapham Yard by the down Windsor local line (adjacent to the up main relief), and at West London junction, three-quarters of a mile east of Clapham, would take one of two sidings each leading to the Yard through a carriage washing plant.

Electric trains from Platforms 16 to 21 bound for Reading, Windsor and the Richmond and Hounslow lines normally took the down Windsor through line, but for just over half a mile from Loco junction, Nine Elms, to Queens Road, Battersea, the two down Windsor lines merge into one; passenger trains normally took precedence at Loco junction, and at busy times a series of empty trains waiting for the road could delay the clearance of platforms at Waterloo.

The engine shed for Waterloo was at Nine Elms (70A), on the down side past Vauxhall (now the site of a fruit and vegetable market). Nearly every steam train leaving Waterloo was hauled by a locomotive which had either been provided by Nine Elms, as in the case of the 09.00 and 15.00 to Plymouth and the 'Atlantic Coast Express' (both sections in summer), or had been turned and serviced there after working in from a country shed on an up train. Engines entered or left the shed by an exit spur

with its own semaphore signal controlled by Loco junction box, and ran into Waterloo on the up through or local line according to traffic; for engines returning from the terminus the down main local line was used more often than not, being adjacent to the shed, during a suitable gap (there were some even in the days of 20-minute interval services to most places) in the suburban departures. When the station was busy engines might run to and from shed in twos and threes to save track occupation.

At the end of Platform 11 there was a small motive power office where a foreman could keep an eye on locomotive and manning problems at the terminus. Some of the Exmouth Junction Pacifics that reached Waterloo during the day were not required again for a considerable time. For instance, the engine of the 10.08 arrival from Yeovil Town at one period returned west on the 18.00 to Plymouth; on the other hand, the Salisbury engines due in at 09.20 and 11.16 left Waterloo at 11.54 and 14.54 respectively.

On the opposite side of the main line to the engine shed, where the London & Southampton Railway's original terminus had been, was Nine Elms Goods, the principal London goods station for the Southern Region Western Section. During the late evening and night there were a number of long-distance freight train departures (and corresponding arrivals) which ran on a separate goods line to Queens Road, Battersea, joining the main line there. During the daytime, however, there was little but local goods traffic in evidence east of Byfleet junction, where the many trains from Feltham marshalling yard joined the main line having travelled via Staines and Virginia Water.

Byfleet junction is one of the burrowing junctions which, together with several flyovers, keep the express lines free from conflicting movements to the extent that there is only one major flat junction (Woking) between Waterloo and Basingstoke. The branches to Epsom, Kingston, and Guildford via Cobham, all burrow under the main line in one direction or the other, the last-named at a spectacular double junction named after the Hampton Court branch whose down track flies over the main line at the same point; the former signalbox also controlled crossovers between through and local lines. Other flyovers are at Durnsford Road, Wimbledon, opposite the electric train depot, where the up local or slow line bridges the down and up through lines so as to be conveniently placed for arrival on the suburban side at Waterloo; and at Pirbright, west of Brookwood, where the up Alton line is carried over the main lines to join the up local line. From Wimbledon to Worting the two local lines are positioned outside the through lines.

The present Waterloo signalbox and Durnsford Road flyover date from 1936, when the layout at the terminus

Right: Some of the Salisbury to Waterloo semi-fast trains called at Surbiton. On 20 May 1961 'Schools' 4-4-0 No 30902 Wellington leaves the up through line platform (No 2) at Surbiton with the 17.15 from Salisbury. Ian J. Turnbull

was altered and the whole area resignalled so as to provide colour-lights as far as Hampton Court junction, 13 miles out. These were four-aspect signals except between Waterloo and Vauxhall where they show only three aspects; on plain track the signals were generally automatic, and many of those at stations and junctions were semi-automatic, controlled by the signalman when necessary.

Thus it became possible to run trains at as little as a two-minute headway between Waterloo and Surbiton (12 miles). On this section the through lines were used, as well as by express trains, by the semi-fast electrics every half-hour to Alton and Portsmouth (first stop Surbiton then all stations, and dividing at Woking); and every 20 minutes to Guildford via Cobham (also stopping at Wimbledon in the off-peak hours). Certain long-distance trains stopped at Surbiton, including the first down and last up West of England expresses of the day. In the down direction there was and is no platform on the through line, and a down express had to switch to the local line and back in order to pick up its passengers.

At Hampton Court junction the abrupt change to semaphore signalling could cause delays, particularly on foggy nights or on a summer Saturday when a fast Portsmouth electric was following a steam train that had left Waterloo only five minutes earlier. The crossovers from down through to down local and up local to up through were frequently used, especially in the rush hour, though not as regularly as those at Surbiton.

Between Hampton Court junction and Woking some of the many stations had platforms on all four lines, others on the local lines only, but express trains seldom stopped on this section. At Esher certain of the Basingstoke and Salisbury semi-fasts, although not stopping before Woking, were regularly switched from the through to the local line in order to keep out of the way of a following West of England express. This applied for example to the 10.54 and 14.54 from Waterloo (and the 18.54 after the introduction of the 19.00 to Plymouth).

The Woking area was resignalled at the time of electrification to Portsmouth in 1937, and colour-lights were provided as far as Brookwood, the next station west on the main line. At the extremely busy junction half a mile beyond Woking station, three electric trains per hour from Portsmouth, plus light engines from Guildford shed and other movements, had to cross the down main line, and it was not always possible to give a clear road to a steam express facing a steady climb for the next seven miles. The 13.00 Waterloo to Plymouth used to stop at Woking to take up only, then running through Basingstoke to its next stop at Andover Junction; and shortly afterwards the 08.15 from Plymouth did the same in the opposite direction. Some stopping trains for the West of England line started or finished their journeys at Woking, such as the 06.33 to Templecombe and certain summer Saturday trains for which there was no room on the tracks to and from Waterloo.

All four lines were electrified as far as Brookwood in those days, for the Aldershot, Farnham and Alton trains; beyond Brookwood only the local lines had conductor rails, and these continued past Pirbright junction to another much less used junction at Sturt Lane, near Farnborough. Here there was a triangular connection on the up side with the electrified line from Aldershot to Ascot; Sturt Lane east curve had some regular traffic, including the unusual 17.37 Waterloo to Ascot via

Left: *Large-chimneyed 'King Arthur' No 30755* The Red Knight *between Brookwood and Farnborough with the 09.54 Waterloo to Southampton Central stopping train on 30 May 1951. The train is passing a gantry of semi-automatic LSWR pneumatic signals under the control of Sturt Lane junction box. On this section the electric conductor rail was on the local lines only, used by a few trains between Woking and Ascot.* E. C. Griffith

Below: *The 15.50 Clapham Junction to Exeter Central milk empties arrives at Basingstoke on the down local line on Sunday 24 June 1956, hauled by Standard Class 5MT No 73110. A stop of 31 minutes was made here on this occasion, during which three more coaches were added. The train was advertised as carrying passengers between Salisbury and Templecombe, and again between Seaton Junction and Exeter Central.* R. C. Riley

Bottom: *The west end of Farnborough station with 'King Arthur' No 30746* Pendragon *awaiting departure on a stopping train to Basingstoke (29 September 1951).* R. D. Swift

Woking (Monday to Friday), headcode 20, but the non-electrified west curve was used only on special occasions in the 1950s, such as engineering diversions or trains to Ascot Races.

From here there were no other junctions until Basingstoke was reached. The signals on this section were automatic semaphore home and distant arms, carried on gantries which spanned all four tracks, signals for up and down lines being on the same gantry. These had been installed by the London & South Western Railway in 1902, and the majority were still lower quadrant. They returned to the 'off' position, worked by air pressure, as soon as a train had cleared the track circuit to the signal in front (or two in front, in the case of distant signals). At stations the signals were semi-automatic, and could be brought under the control of the signalbox.

Basingstoke, a stopping station for about half the regular West of England expresses, had four through platforms and two bays, an engine shed, whose duties were mainly mixed traffic and local, three signalboxes, three goods yards and a set of carriage sidings. At the London end is the important junction with the Western Region line to Reading, formerly controlled by C box, carrying traffic from the Midlands and North to Southampton, Bournemouth and Portsmouth, and the up bay was used mainly for starting trains to Reading. The other bay was at the west end next to the down local platform, and was used for example by the engine and coaches of the 12.54 Waterloo to Basingstoke which, having unloaded in the down local platform, ran into the bay to form the 14.48 stopping train to Salisbury.

At Worting junction, 2.5 miles to the west, the through lines pass beneath Battledown flyover to become the West of England line, and the local tracks, on the outside, become the Bournemouth line, the flyover carrying the up Bournemouth line over the West of England lines. The crossovers at Worting allow a train in either direction to switch from through to local line or vice versa, and in the 1950s a down express for Bournemouth or the West of England generally remained on the through line to

Worting, but some down Bournemouth expresses stopping at Basingstoke changed to the local line there. Conversely, many stopping trains bound for Salisbury changed to the through line at Basingstoke. Nevertheless it sometimes happened that a Bournemouth train was approaching Worting on the through line at the same time as a Salisbury train was approaching on the local line, and one would of course have to be checked.

Worting junction to Andover Junction

Beyond Worting the West of England line changed its character. There were mostly country stations with small goods yards, occasional milk depots, and signal posts as opposed to gantries. Whereas in the 1970s only three other passenger lines joined or crossed the main line between here and Exeter Central, 20 years ago there were 11. The first was at Whitchurch, where there were two stations, Whitchurch North on the main line and Whitchurch Town on the Didcot, Newbury & Southampton line. The latter passed beneath the main line close to Whitchurch North station, and there was no connection between the two.

Andover Junction to Salisbury

At Andover Junction the main line was crossed by the former Midland & South Western Junction route linking Cheltenham and Southampton. There were two through trains a day in each direction between these towns, hauled mostly by 'Manor' 4-6-0s from Gloucester or one of Eastleigh's 'U' class 2-6-0s. Other trains left Andover Junction for Western Region territory such as Swindon, Marlborough or (while the branch from Ludgershall remained opened to passengers) Tidworth; the Tidworth

Below: *Class T9 No 30724 propels an empty Bulleid three-coach set in Barton Mill sidings, east of Basingstoke on the up side, on August Bank Holiday 1958. These sidings are now used for stabling electric units.* M. Mensing

Above: *WR 'Hall' class No 6953* Leighton Hall *takes the Reading line at Basingstoke with the 10.07 stopping train from Southampton Terminus on 28 April 1962. This junction was controlled by Basingstoke C box.* Colin P. Walker

Right: *'King Arthur' No 30799* Sir Ironside, *recently transferred to Salisbury shed from Bricklayers Arms because of the Kent Coast electrification (it does not appear to have received its new shedplate), leaves the down through platform at Basingstoke on a Saturday in summer 1959 with the 16.48 stopping train to Yeovil Town. The engine still carries the reporting number of its previous working, the 14.54 Waterloo to Basingstoke (hence the '2.54' chalked on the number board for the guidance of the man at Waterloo who had the job of attaching each number to the correct train).* P. Ransome-Wallis

Bottom right: *No 34029* Lundy *of Exmouth Junction shed, having worked up to London on the 06.30 Exeter Central slow, returns west with the milk empties from Clapham Junction. Photographed near Andover on 8 April 1952.* B. E. Coates

trains were mainly worked by a Western Region '45xx' tank or a Southern 'M7' 0-4-4T, those to and from Swindon by a 'Manor' or a '43xx' 2-6-0. Southern trains reached Andover Junction from Eastleigh, Portsmouth & Southsea, and Southampton Terminus, and once daily from Fawley and Weymouth. Classes T9 and U, and the Standard tank engines and 2-6-0s hauled these trains. At the end of 1957 'Hampshire' diesel units were introduced, of two coaches, later increased to three, and covered all the trains to Andover from Portsmouth and Eastleigh, running at approximately regular intervals.

The line from the Southampton direction via Romsey, Stockbridge and Andover Town joined the main line at Andover Junction itself, where there was a bay on the down side for terminating trains. On the main line Andover Junction had one platform line for down trains, but in the up direction there were both a platform line and a through line, so that an up train stopping at the station could be overtaken by an express. The through trains to and from the Cheltenham line normally used the outer face of the up platform, whether northbound or southbound, and between Andover and the junction at Redpost or Red Posts, two miles to the west, kept to their own single track, used in both directions, adjacent to the main line. Beyond Redpost the ex-Midland & South Western Junction line was double track, as was the Southern line to Andover Junction from Romsey.

At Newton Tony, west of Grateley, two spurs from the main line joined to form the branch to Amesbury and Bulford. Trains for the branch from the east used a separate single track from Grateley which ran parallel for some way with the main line; from the Salisbury direction they diverged at Amesbury junction signalbox, where a burrowing junction enabled trains from Amesbury to Salisbury to reach the down main line without crossing the up line. The branch had double track as far as Amesbury and single on to Bulford, where it extended beyond the village to the army camp. In the late 1940s there were seven passenger trains a day in each direction between Salisbury and Bulford, and on Sunday evenings a

Above: Standard Class 3MT tank engine No 82020 awaits departure from the MSWJ platform at Andover Junction on 23 July 1961 with the Sunday 20.35 to Swindon. W. Sumner

Top right: On 8 July 1956 'Merchant Navy' class No 35020 Bibby Line leaves the up main platform at Andover Junction with the Sunday 14.50 Plymouth Friary to Waterloo, which made further intermediate stops at Basingstoke, Woking and Surbiton. The engine is working Nine Elms duty 2, and the train number 224 will have been affixed at Salisbury; train numbers were carried by all regular steam trains due into Waterloo on a summer Sunday evening between 17.00 and midnight. On the left of the engine is the up through line, and next to that the buffers of the down middle siding. R. C. Riley

Centre right: On 14 May 1955 Class U 2-6-0 No 31634 passes Andover Junction West box with an up freight. The train is signalled into the platform line and is about to terminate. The engine was shedded at Basingstoke and is working duty number 242. R. C. Riley

Bottom right: No 31634 and its train can just be seen in the platform, prior to shunting into the goods yard, as 'King Arthur' No 30779 Sir Colgrevance departs for all stations to Salisbury with the 11.54 from Waterloo. R. C. Riley

through train from Waterloo for soldiers returning from weekend leave. But for the last year before the complete closure of the western spur in 1952 there was only one passenger train a day from Bulford to Salisbury and back, consisting of an 'M7' tank engine and usually one coach. The branch remained open until 1963 for military specials and freight via the east curve from Grateley. The special troop trains were often hauled by Bulleid light Pacifics, the only large engines permitted to run to the end of the branch.

Salisbury

All passenger trains, except the 'Devon Belle', stopped at Salisbury, which is just under half way from Waterloo to Exeter. The regular expresses changed crews here, and

their engines took water; this was the terminus for the majority of main line stopping trains from either direction. On ordinary days (until the 19.00 Waterloo to Plymouth was introduced) the only nonstop runs between Waterloo and Salisbury were by the down and up 'Atlantic Coast Express'.

The main line meets at Salisbury the important cross-country route from Portsmouth and Southampton to Bristol and Cardiff, operated by the Southern Region to the south of Salisbury and by the Western Region to the north. Through trains between the South Coast and Bristol or beyond invariably changed engines here. This line approached from the direction of Romsey, and at Alderbury junction, five miles from Salisbury, was joined by the single track from Bournemouth via Fordingbridge. After passing the goods depot at Milford the South Coast line joined the Waterloo line at Salisbury Tunnel junction (so called to distinguish it from Tunnel junction at Southampton). Some trains from this direction terminated in the bay platform (Number 6) at the east end of Salisbury station on the down side. Salisbury has four through platforms, in pairs, two for each direction. The Bristol line was connected only with the northern platform of each pair, Numbers 1 (up) and 3 (down); cross-country trains used these platforms and London trains normally kept to Numbers 2 and 4.

The principal trains to reach Salisbury from the Romsey direction were the two daily through trains from Brighton, to Cardiff and Plymouth respectively. These services in both directions called at Salisbury in the space of just over two hours in the early afternoon. Brighton shed was responsible for working these trains to Salisbury and back, and although they were normally rostered for 'West Country' Pacifics, a wide variety of engines was used at different times in the 1950s, including the Maunsell Moguls, 4-4-0s of Classes L, T9 and L12, the Brighton Atlantics, and even Standard 2-6-4T engines.

There were a number of through trains each day between Portsmouth and Bristol or Cardiff, both semi-fast and slow, and stopping trains reached Salisbury from Bournemouth (usually West), Portsmouth (via Eastleigh or Southampton Central) and Southampton Terminus. The 'T9' class and the Standard 2-6-0s were common on both the Fordingbridge line and the Romsey line in the 1950s, while the latter also saw, among other types, the 'D15' 4-4-0s and 'U' class 2-6-0s. As on the Andover line, the local steam trains between Portsmouth and Salisbury were replaced by an hourly service of 'Hampshire' diesel units at the end of 1957.

At the height of the summer an excursion train ran on weekdays along the Fordingbridge line to Weymouth and back, and later in the 1950s a similar train served Swanage, while for one season there was a through excursion to Littlehampton via Fareham and Havant. After the newspaper train from Waterloo had called at about three in the morning, two connecting trains left Salisbury, one for stations to Yeovil Town and the other

Below: *'Battle of Britain' class No 34052* Lord Dowding *leaves Bishopdown tunnel and passes Salisbury Tunnel junction with a London express. Trains to Portsmouth, Southampton and Bournemouth took the lines leading to the left behind the signalbox.* W. Philip Conolly

Top right: *Standard Class 9F 2-10-0 No 92136 takes water in Platform 3 at Salisbury with an oil train from Fawley to the Western Region.* P. Hutchinson

Centre right: *Trains to and from the Western Region could only use Platforms 1 and 3 at Salisbury. Class 94xx 0-6-0PT No 8479, deputising for the more usual 2-8-2T, passes through Platform 1 on 14 August 1959 with a freight from Severn Tunnel junction to Salisbury East Yard.* D. Fereday Glenn

Bottom right: *'Modified Hall' No 6981* Marbury Hall *leaves Salisbury for Cardiff with the Sunday 14.03 from Portsmouth & Southsea on 5 October 1952. The engine shed is on the extreme right.* G. F. Heiron

Above: *On 2 July 1954 Class 72xx 2-8-2T No 7205 approaches Salisbury on the Westbury line with a freight. The lamp headcode denotes a mineral train, probably coal from South Wales.* Brian E. Morrison

Below: *Class S15 No 30830 leaves the up reception road at Salisbury with a banana train from Bristol which it has just taken over from a Western Region engine. The disc headcode indicates Southampton Docks via Eastleigh. Photographed at 13.15 on 21 May 1953.* A. C. V. Kendall

Above: *The junction between the Salisbury to Exeter main line and the line to Westbury and Bristol was formerly at the west end of Salisbury station and controlled by C signalbox. On a busy Saturday in 1957, 27 July, WR Class 28xx 2-8-0 No 2863, of Aberdare shed, has been turned out for passenger duty on a relief from Cardiff to Bournemouth, and is passing C box on its way to Platform 1 where it will be relieved by a Southern Region engine. The connection from Platform 3 to the down Westbury line can be seen making a diamond crossing with the up Exeter line on the left.* J. A. Young

Below: *The 15.00 Waterloo to Plymouth arrives at Salisbury on 28 August 1964 behind 'Merchant Navy' No 35025 Brocklebank Line. In the down bay, connecting with the express, is the 16.54 stopping train to Templecombe with a Maunsell 2-6-0 in charge (this was a turn for a Yeovil 'U' class).* R. A. Lumber

for Weymouth via Fordingbridge. An early morning departure from Salisbury's east bay was the unadvertised train to Idmiston Halt for workers at Porton Down research establishment; the tank engine and two coaches went on empty to Grateley and spent the day in a siding until the return trip. Other trains joining the main line at Tunnel junction were transfer freights between Milford goods depot and the East or West Yards at Salisbury.

At the west end of the station is another bay platform on the down side (Number 5), formerly used for local trains starting at Salisbury. The Bristol line diverged immediately west of the platforms but kept close to the Exeter line as far as Wilton; the Western Region had its own station, Wilton North, which was closed in 1955, the Southern station (made famous by the 'Devon Belle' engine change) being Wilton South. After 1955 Warminster, 20 miles away, was the first station open on the Westbury line; the majority of trains on this section ran to and from the South Coast, but there were occasional stopping trains between Salisbury and Bristol, Cardiff or Swindon.

Templecombe

Templecombe, where the Somerset & Dorset line from Bath to Bournemouth crossed the main line, was once the scene of some fascinating railway operations. Much has been published, in words and pictures, about the Somerset & Dorset, and suffice it here to give a brief description of Templecombe itself. Coming from Bournemouth, the Somerset & Dorset was single track, except at stations, from Blandford to Templecombe; and double track from Templecombe almost to Bath. Near the bridge by which the single track passed under the Waterloo main line was a platform called Templecombe Lower, but almost all Somerset & Dorset trains stopping at Templecombe used their own platform at the upper or main line station, reached by a double track spur from Templecombe No 2

junction, on the north side of the station near the engine shed. Northbound and southbound trains entered the station from the same direction and used the same platform, which was on the outer side of the up Waterloo platform. Northbound trains calling at Templecombe had to be hauled up the spur into the station by a pilot engine while the train engine pushed from behind; southbound trains had to be hauled backwards out of the station. It was permitted to move two trains together from the station to the junction, coupled end to end, with the engines of course on the outside, and send them on their separate ways at the bottom. In the 1950s this happened

Below: *Templecombe No 2 junction looking south. A Saturday extra from Bournemouth West to Huddersfield via the Somerset & Dorset line, hauled by Class 7F 2-8-0 No 53805, has passed Templecombe Lower and under the Waterloo main line and has just reached Templecombe No 2 junction where the points are set for it to cross to the northbound track. On the extreme left Templecombe shed can just be seen, and above the last three coaches the double track spur leading to the Southern station. 13 August 1960.* Ivo Peters

Top right: *Templecombe No 2 junction looking north. On 7 July 1961 Class 9F 2-10-0 No 92001 takes the spur from No 2 junction to the Upper station with a stopping train from Bristol to Bournemouth West.* Michael J. Fox

Centre right: *The four tracks through Yeovil Junction are shown in this picture of 'Merchant Navy' class No 35022* Holland-America Line *making its booked stop with the 10.48 Torrington to Waterloo on Saturday 13 July 1963. This was the second part of the 'Atlantic Coast Express', and Salisbury will be its only intermediate stop before London.* Ian J. Turnbull

Bottom right: *A through freight has stopped at the down main platform at Yeovil Junction, probably for water, on 22 July 1958. The engine is 'Battle of Britain' class No 34069* Hawkinge. R. C. Riley

regularly just after 09.00 with a Bournemouth to Bath train and a Bristol to Bournemouth train.

Except at holiday periods the 'Pines Express', from Bournemouth to Manchester, Liverpool and Sheffield, and a mid-morning train from Bournemouth to Gloucester (later Bristol) were the only regular Somerset & Dorset passenger trains to omit the stop at Templecombe. A late night stopping train from Bournemouth on Saturdays terminated at the Lower platform and was worked empty to Templecombe Upper. Apart from the Somerset & Dorset platform the station had a simple layout of down and up main line platforms, and an extensive goods yard to the west. The engine shed, on the lower level, had belonged to the Somerset & Dorset, and in the 1950s almost all the engines allocated to Templecombe were for use on that line; for some years, however, one of the large Class Z 0-8-0Ts was based at Templecombe for shunting in the main line goods yard and occasional piloting of passenger trains to and from the Somerset & Dorset.

Yeovil

In the 1950s Yeovil had three stations, all interconnected. There was Pen Mill on the former Great Western line to Weymouth (then double track throughout), which passes under the Waterloo to Exeter line east of Yeovil Junction. The Southern station on the main line at Yeovil Junction (a mile and a half from the middle of the town) had two island platforms, the inside faces of which served as through platforms for down and up main line trains. Between these were through lines for each direction, used by expresses passing Yeovil nonstop (Yeovil Junction and Seaton Junction were the only places between Salisbury

and Exeter Central where a stopping train could be overtaken by an express without being shunted). On the up side at Yeovil Junction was a bay platform used mainly by the frequent service of push-and-pull trains to and from Yeovil Town. This service, worked by an 'M7' tank engine, used a pair of tracks which left Yeovil Junction in the up direction, ran parallel with the Western Region line for a short distance, and then curved round to enter Yeovil Town station from the east. A single track connected Yeovil Town and Pen Mill stations, and was used mainly by the Taunton trains, which called at Yeovil Town and terminated at Pen Mill.

The Bristol & Exeter Railway reached Yeovil by a branch from Taunton via Martock six years before the completion of the line from Salisbury to Exeter, and Yeovil Town was opened as a joint station in 1861. In the 1950s it had three running lines and an engine shed. One line, with a platform on both sides, was used mainly by the Taunton to Pen Mill trains; the other two, each with a platform, by Southern trains. Besides the push-and-pull service from Yeovil Junction, some main line stopping trains started or terminated at Yeovil Town. These had to work to Yeovil Junction and then, if proceeding towards

Below: *'Battle of Britain' No 34055* Fighter Pilot *leaves the up main platform at Yeovil Junction on 22 July 1958 with a train believed to be the 16.35 Exeter Central to Salisbury stopper. No 34055 has taken over at Yeovil Junction from a 'Merchant Navy' class, and in the bay a Class M7 waits with the Yeovil Town auto train. As can be seen from the signal gantry, the up through line, up platform line and up bay each gave access to both the main line to Salisbury and the branch to Yeovil Town.* R. C. Riley

Above: *When propelling, the headcode disc was carried on the front coach, and the tail lamp on the engine's buffer beam of the Yeovil Town auto train. On Sunday 2 August 1959 'M7' No 30131 passes Yeovil South junction with the 10.18 from Yeovil Town, a service put on in the summer to connect with a Sunday excursion train from Salisbury to Exeter which itself connected with branch trains to all the East Devon resorts. The driver can be seen in the front cab of ex-LSWR gated set No 373, and the pair of tracks in the foreground is the Castle Cary to Weymouth line.* S. C. Nash

Below: *Still on duty 517 a year later, but with a more modern push-and-pull set, No 30131 stands in the up main platform at Yeovil Junction on 9 September 1960.* N. M. Lera

Above: *A Sunday view of Yeovil Town station, carriage sidings and engine shed on 25 August 1957, with the Yeovil Junction push-and-pull train in Platforms 1 and 2. The track between Platforms 1 and 2 was used mainly by the Western Region's Yeovil (Pen Mill) to Taunton trains, except on Sundays when there was no service on this line.* C. P. Boocock

Below: *Yeovil Town on August Bank Holiday 1957. WR Class 51xx 2-6-2T No 4133 (left) is arriving in Platform 1 with the empty coaches for an excursion to Weymouth, which it will have to run round and haul back to Pen Mill, where it has just come from. In Platform 2 Class U No 31795 awaits departure with an eight-coach excursion to the East Devon resorts, while No 30131 and the push-and-pull set have been relegated to a siding (extreme right).* R. A. Lumber

Salisbury, reverse; the engine of an eastbound train ran tender-first from Yeovil Town to Yeovil Junction, or in some cases backed on to the train at Yeovil Junction, a different engine having brought the train from Yeovil Town. Three main line trains left Yeovil Town in the morning before 08.00, two for Ilfracombe and one for Waterloo. The Waterloo train became an express after Tisbury and ran nonstop from Basingstoke; it had a slower counterpart down in the evening. There was also the through coach for Waterloo which left Yeovil Town at lunchtime coupled to the auto train; at Yeovil Junction it was attached to a stopping train to Salisbury, where it was finally placed at the back of the up 'Atlantic Coast Express'.

Allocated to Yeovil (Southern Region) engine shed were some of the 'U' class, and the engines for the Yeovil Junction auto train. There was also a Western Region engine shed at Yeovil, near Pen Mill station, with an allocation of '45xx' and '57xx' tank engines; in 1959 it was closed and its engines transferred to the Southern shed.

At Yeovil South junction signalbox, between the Junction and Town stations, a connection had been laid during World War 2 to allow through running between Yeovil Junction and Pen Mill, but it saw no regular service in the 1950s. A traveller between, say, Exeter and Dorchester usually had to change at all three Yeovil stations, although one or two of the Weymouth to Pen Mill auto trains reversed and ran to Yeovil Town and back.

In the down direction a main line stopping train could connect with an express at Yeovil Junction, by shunting into the bay line (normally used for vans) at the outer face of the down platform, but then had to shunt back to the down platform before departing. For instance the 17.00 from Waterloo, although carrying Yeovil Junction destination boards, was a through train to Exeter (the restaurant car was not staffed beyond Yeovil); it was scheduled to wait for some 40 minutes at Yeovil Junction while the 18.00 Waterloo to Plymouth called at the station and departed first.

Chard Junction

The single track branch from Chard Junction to Taunton had been owned by the Southern Railway as far as Chard Central and by the Great Western beyond, Chard Central being a joint station. In the 1950s the branch, although in Southern Region territory, was operated throughout by the Western Region. Passengers from the main line at Chard Junction had to cross the station approach road to reach the branch platform, where they normally found a 0-6-0PT or one of the larger '45xx' 2-6-2T engines and a Western Region two-coach 'B' set. Most trains ran between Chard Junction and Taunton, but as a rule there was a lengthy wait at Chard Central, since this was the only regular crossing point and branch services were generally timed to connect with main line trains at either end.

The branch platform at Chard Junction was a terminus, and the only connection with the main line was

Below: *On Good Friday 1957, with a Sunday service in force, 'King Arthur' No 30450* Sir Kay *leaves Yeovil Town with the 11.48 to Salisbury. At Yeovil Junction the 'King Arthur' will run round its train, and the headcode discs for forward working are already in position. Behind the engine can be seen the single track to Pen Mill.* R. A. Lumber

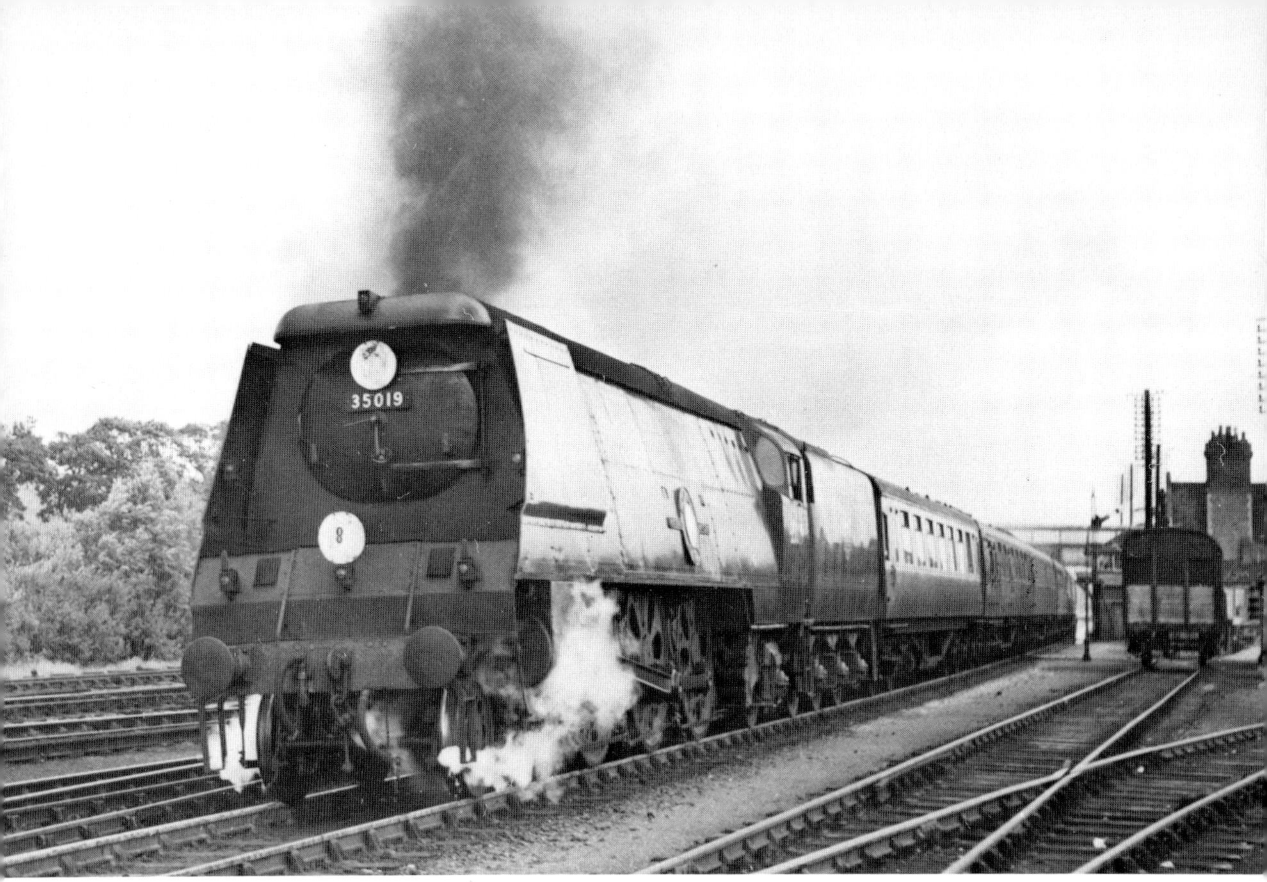
35019

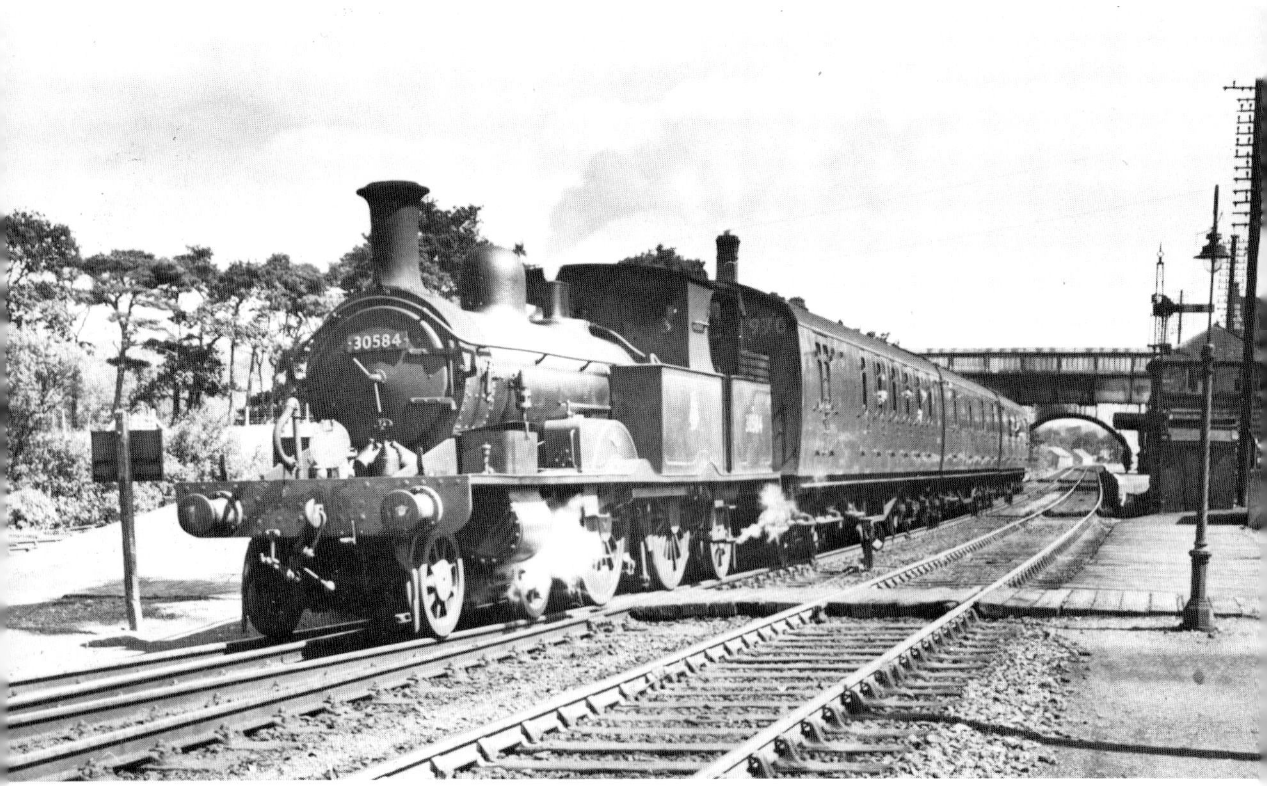
30584

Above left: *'Merchant Navy' class No 35019* French Line CGT *leaves Axminster with a Sunday Waterloo to Plymouth train on 26 August 1956.* L. Marshall

Left: *At Axminster it was not possible to reach the Lyme Regis branch direct from the main line. On Saturday 11 July 1959 the 08.05 Waterloo to Exmouth has detached three Lyme Regis coaches in the down platform (on right) and departed. No 30584 has picked up the coaches and shunted them to the up platform, and is beginning another shunt movement into the branch bay. Here the through coaches were coupled in front of the two-coach branch set which had arrived from Lyme Regis behind No 30583, and both engines hauled the combined train to the branch terminus.* R. C. Riley

Above: *One coach was usually sufficient for the Lyme Regis branch train except in the summer. Here No 30582 stands in the bay platform at Axminster with the branch train.* J. Davenport

by shunting into the goods yard. There were no regular through coaches from the main line to the branch in the 1950s, but the connection was used by occasional excursion trains, for instance from Taunton to Seaton.

Axminster

Axminster was the junction for the first of several branches to the coast, which set a steep and twisting course for $6\frac{3}{4}$ miles to Lyme Regis. The branch was opened in 1903, having been constructed under a Light Railway Order (which meant that it did not have to meet the same engineering requirements as a railway authorised by Act of Parliament), and left Axminster from a bay platform on the up side, then crossing by a bridge over the main line. The curves were severe, and the gradients as steep as 1 in 40. The track was single throughout, the one intermediate station at Combpyne no longer having a crossing loop in the 1950s; there was an overall speed limit of 25mph and the journey time of 21 minutes to Lyme Regis was only five minutes quicker than by bus.

To work the branch needed an engine of some power, a flexible wheelbase, and not too great a load on each axle. Just before World War 1, the London & South-Western Railway tried an Adams 4-4-2 radial tank, of a class built in the 1880s for the outer suburbs of London, and as a result these engines had a virtual monopoly of the branch until 1961. For most of the period between the wars there were two engines, working the branch for a week in turn, and in 1946 the Southern Railway bought a third from a private railway company. On Nationalisation they were numbered 30582-4 (and No 30583 is still in steam on the Bluebell Railway).

Because of their suitability for the Lyme Regis branch, these three engines outlived the rest of their class by about 30 years. From time to time, especially when they became due for overhaul, other types were tried without success. Finally, work began in 1960 to realign some of the sharp bends, and then London Midland Region 2-6-2Ts took over the line for a few years.

Left: *By 5 April 1961 the '0415' class had almost reached the end of its service on the branch. No 30583 has brought one coach from Lyme Regis bunker first and is running round at Axminster for the next down working.* R. N. Joanes

Below left: *The end of the branch engine's runround loop is visible in this picture of No 30584 curving away from the main line at Axminster with two ex-LSWR non-corridors on 18 June 1949.* S. C. Nash

Below: *On Sunday 30 August 1953 No 30584 nears Axminster with the 12.33 from Lyme Regis.* S. C. Nash

Above: *An evening stopping train departs from the down platform at Seaton Junction behind 'Battle of Britain' class No 34050* Royal Observer Corps. *The Seaton branch platform can be seen on the extreme right.* F. R. Hebron

Below: *The 14.06 to Seaton departs from Seaton Junction on 30 July 1960 propelled by Class M7 No 30125* R. A. Lumber

The Lyme Regis branch train consisted of one or two coaches. In the summer the through coach from London (detached at Templecombe from the 13.00 Waterloo) was uncoupled at Axminster from the Templecombe to Exeter stopping train and left in the down platform. The branch engine collected the coach and, by means of a double shunting movement via the up line and a siding, added it to the front of its train in the bay. In the up direction the through coach in summer left Lyme Regis on the branch train at 11.37, travelled from Axminster to Salisbury at the back of the 08.55 Ilfracombe stopping train, and there, with the through Yeovil Town coach, was attached to the 'Atlantic Coast Express' (the first section on days when that train was divided).

Seaton Junction

The branch line to Seaton was the shortest and, starting where the main line is in a dip, the least hilly of the coastal branches, and the only one worked by a push-pull train. It was just over four miles long and a single track, with stations at Colyton and Colyford but no crossing points. The train generally consisted of two coaches in winter and three in summer, and 'M7' tank engines worked up and down this line for 30 years until 1963. The through Waterloo coach was attached to the push-and-pull set for its journey along the branch. Seaton Junction, after being rebuilt in 1928, had four tracks, a through line and a platform line in each direction, and the branch train left in the up direction from a bay set at a wide angle to the down platform.

Above: The 08.30 Padstow to Waterloo, with through coaches from Bude, leaves Seaton Junction on its nonstop run to Salisbury on Saturday 11 July 1959. The engine, No 35008 Orient Line, and the front five or six coaches including restaurant car, have come on at Exeter Central.   R. C. Riley

Sidmouth Junction

The Sidmouth branch also left the main line in an easterly direction and, passing through Ottery St Mary, came to another junction at Tipton St John, where the branch to Exmouth via Budleigh Salterton diverged to the right. Both branches were single track and had some steep climbing at gradients of 1 in 45 to 1 in 50. The basic train formation was two non-corridor coaches, and the engine diagrams were interworked with those on the Exeter to Exmouth branch which met the line from Tipton St John outside Exmouth station. During the 1950s the Drummond 'M7s' were gradually being replaced by the larger BR Standard and LMR 2-6-2Ts, but in the early years the older Adams 0-4-4Ts were still to be seen.

Sidmouth Junction had an up and down main line platform and a bay on the down side for branch trains. The through coaches from Waterloo to Exmouth and Sidmouth travelled via Tipton St John, where joining and dividing took place. Some branch trains ran between Exeter Central and Sidmouth via Sidmouth Junction, and some between Exmouth and Sidmouth by reversing at Tipton St John. For example, the through coach from

Exmouth to Waterloo departed at 09.52 on a train bound for Sidmouth. At Tipton St John it was transferred to the 10.20 Sidmouth to Exeter (which included the through Sidmouth to Waterloo coach), and eventually at Sidmouth Junction it was attached to a train travelling in the right direction, the 08.15 Plymouth to Waterloo. When the 08.15 Plymouth reached Sidmouth Junction the express engine had to leave its train to collect the coaches from Exmouth and Sidmouth and attach them to the front.

Tank engine-hauled trains ran on the main line between Exeter Central and Honiton, mainly in the morning and evening, and there was a return journey at midday from Exeter to Broad Clyst, less than five miles away. The 08.00 train from Exeter provided the engine to shunt Honiton goods yard all day, and in the afternoon during school terms a Sidmouth branch train was extended from Sidmouth Junction to Honiton for pupils returning from King's School, Ottery St Mary, and returned empty.

Exeter

On the outskirts of the city is Exmouth Junction, once famous for an engine shed second in importance only to Nine Elms, now merely, as its name implies, the junction for the Exmouth branch. Exmouth Junction shed, or 72A, had about eight 'Merchant Navy' Pacifics for hauling the

Below: Standard 2-6-2T No 82025 has arrived bunker-first at Budleigh Salterton on 9 July 1959 with the 14.50 from Exmouth, which terminates there. No 82025 has then run round via the single line crossing loop (on right) and is backing on to the other end of its train to form the 15.20 back to Exmouth. R. C. Riley

Right: In the summer of 1964 Nine Elms duty 15 on Saturdays for a 'Merchant Navy' class was to work the 09.00 Waterloo to Exmouth as far as Sidmouth Junction and return home on the Okehampton to Surbiton Car-Carrier. On 15 August No 35028 Clan Line arrives at Sidmouth Junction with the 09.00 Waterloo. Here No 35028 will be detached and will immediately run light to Exmouth Junction shed for servicing. One or two tank engines will back on to the other end of the train and haul the combined Sidmouth and Exmouth portions as far as Tipton St John where the two branches diverge. By 1964 the regular branch service had been taken over by Western Region dmus, one of which can just be seen in the bay. Ian G. Holt

Centre right: Standard 2-6-2T No 82019 leaves Sidmouth on 13 July 1959 in charge of the 10.20 to Exeter Central, with a through coach for Waterloo at the rear. At Tipton St John a through coach from Exmouth to Waterloo will be added, and at Sidmouth Junction both coaches will be transferred to the front of the 08.25 Plymouth to Waterloo express. R. C. Riley

Bottom right: Class M7 No 30044 shunts at Sidmouth Junction on 1 September 1958. The main line is behind the engine and can be seen on the extreme left, while the Sidmouth branch goes out of the picture to the right. K. L. Cook

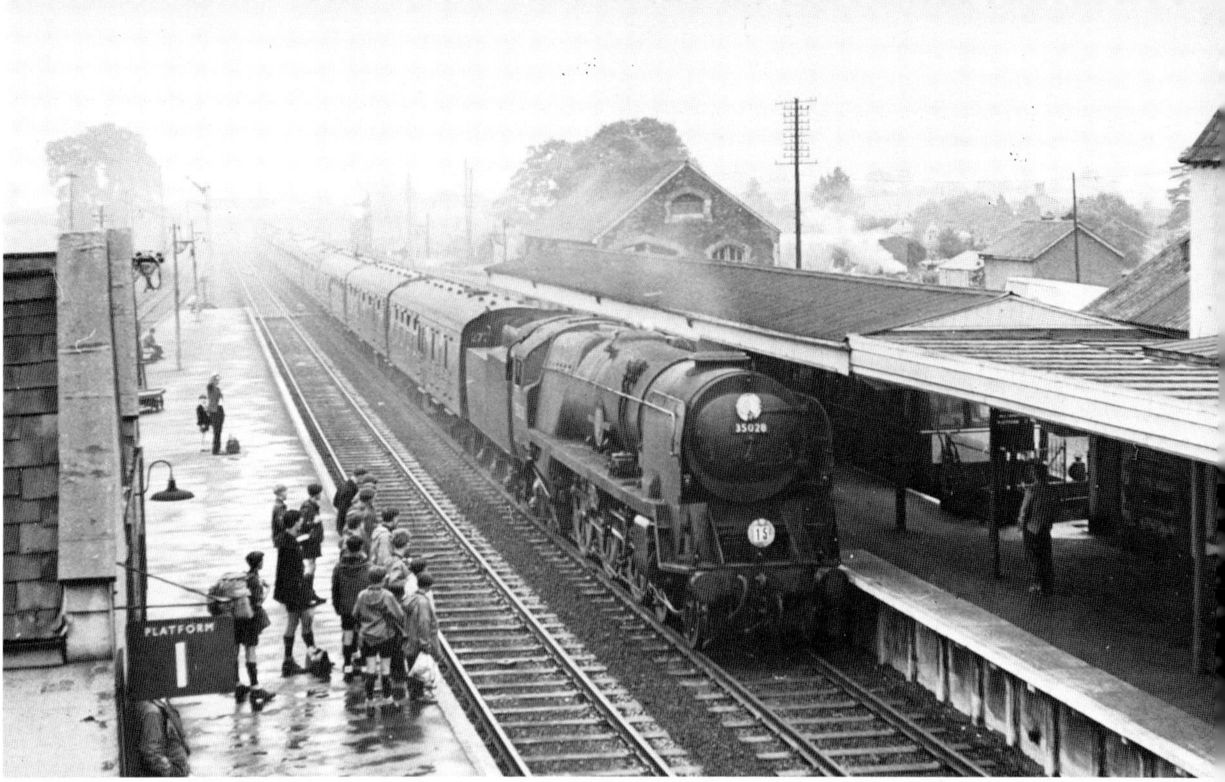
PLATFORM
1
35028

24

30044

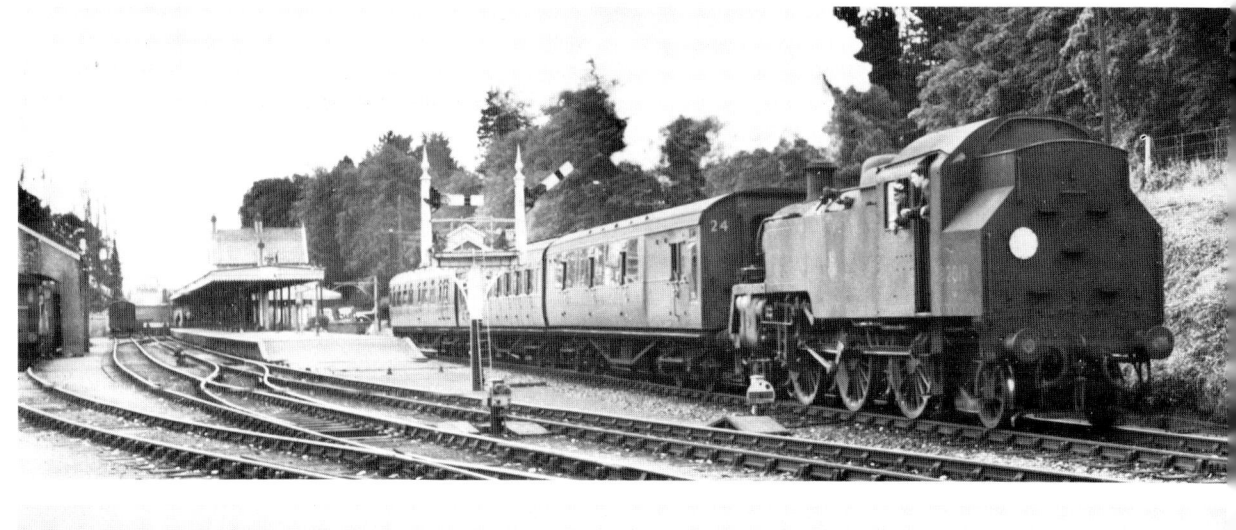

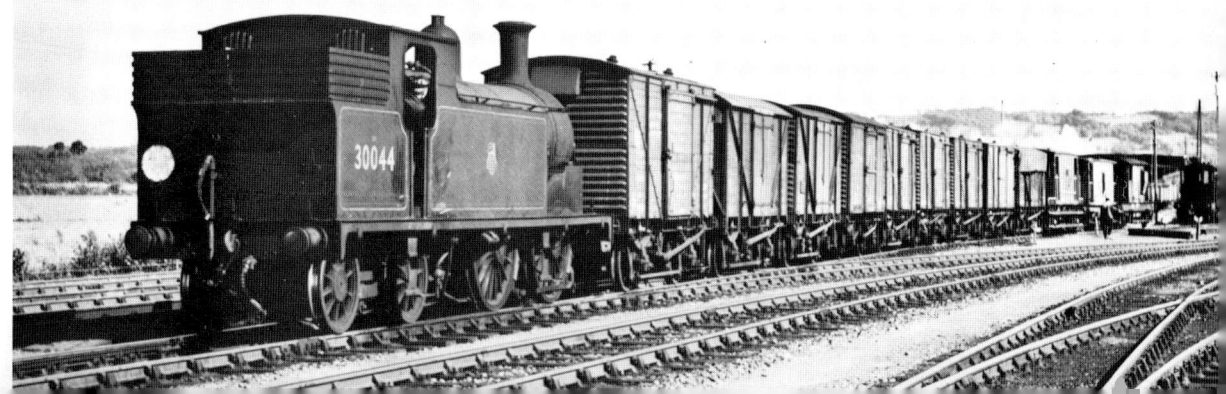

expresses between Waterloo and Exeter, 25 to 30 light Pacifics, employed both east and west of Exeter, plus main line freight engines, chiefly 'S15' 4-6-0s, the Exeter banking, shunting and local passenger engines, and the tank engines for the Lyme Regis and Seaton branches (although when on duty these spent the night at their subsheds).

Before the Exeter to Exmouth branch was opened in 1861, rail travellers reached Exmouth by ferry from Starcross on the Great Western. Leaving the main line in the up direction at Exmouth Junction, the branch was double track as far as Topsham, about half-way to Exmouth, and single from there on. In the 1950s trains were mostly three or four coaches in winter outside the peak hours, but up to seven at busier times. An up train in the morning stopped only at Topsham, and in 1960 a down evening nonstop train was introduced.

Exeter Central station, gloomily overshadowed by Rougemont Castle on one side and the prison on the other, had two main platform lines with two through lines between, and on the outer face of each platform was a bay for Exmouth trains. Normally trains from Waterloo detached their restaurant cars here, and were divided into Plymouth and Ilfracombe sections, which set off one after

Below: Exmouth Junction. 'Battle of Britain' class No 34062 17 Squadron passes the engine shed and marshalling yard at the head of an up express. R. Russell

Bottom: The Saturday 10.35 Waterloo to Padstow and Bude enters the down platform at Exeter Central on 1 August 1964. 'Battle of Britain' class No 34057 Biggin Hill has worked through from Waterloo and will be replaced by Class N 2-6-0 No 31859, and at the same time the rear two coaches will be detached. In the foreground is the scissors crossover between the up through and up platform lines. R. A. Lumber

Top: *The 13.15 Exeter Central to Exmouth climbs towards St James' Park Halt on 19 August 1961 hauled by Standard 2-6-2T No 82017.* W. L. Underhay

Above: *This time No 82017 is seen leaving Exmouth on 13 July 1959 with a three-coach non-corridor set forming the 13.45 to Exeter Central.* R. C. Riley

the other although travelling for some distance on the same metals. Midway along the up platform line was a scissors connection with the up through line, to help the marshalling of London-bound expresses. On a typical occasion a light Pacific would arrive first with the Plymouth portion, stop with its train well forward of the scissors, and leave for the shed. The station pilot, waiting on the up through line with the restaurant and tavern cars, would then propel these to the rear of the Plymouth coaches over the scissor crossing. About this time the 'Merchant Navy' for the London run would have backed on to the front of the train. When the portion from Ilfracombe and Torrington arrived, its light Pacific would leave the platform by way of the scissors, and the 'Merchant Navy' would finally back its coaches down to complete the train. In this way the restaurant car was placed in the middle of the train, although coming down from Waterloo it had to be near the back. In the summer, when some up trains ran in two parts, the express engine would usually collect the restaurant car portion and back it on to the front, since the train was otherwise complete on arrival at Exeter Central.

Above: *In the 1950s the summer service did not generally begin until mid-June. On 14 June 1959 the winter timetable was in its final day of operation as No 34052 Lord Dowding approached Exeter Central with the Sunday 12.27 Portsmouth & Southsea to Plymouth. Behind are a restaurant car and a tavern car, probably not needed until the next day.*
M. Mensing

Left: *The facade of Exeter Central in the 1960s, bearing the sign 'Through expresses to Salisbury, London, Portsmouth, Brighton, Plymouth, North Devon and North Cornwall'. In 1979 this remained true as regards Salisbury, London, Brighton (on Saturdays) and North Devon (ie Barnstaple).*
R. A. Lumber

Bottom left: *The Ilfracombe and Torrington coaches of the 10.30 Exeter Central to Waterloo climb the 1 in 37 out of Exeter St Davids behind 'Battle of Britain' No 34074 46 Squadron. They will be followed by a portion from Plymouth, and more coaches will be added at Sidmouth Junction. The engine is one of those displaced from the Kent Coast in the late 1950s.* Colin P. Walker

Top: *Photographed from the down platform, 'King Arthur' No 30452* Sir Meliagrance *passes Exeter Central on the up through line on 3 July 1958 with a train of stone hoppers.* J. Scrace

Above: *The best-known Exeter bankers were the Class E1 radial tanks, of which No 32695 is seen piloting Class N No 31831 out of Platform 3 at Exeter St Davids on an up freight in April 1953.* P. Ransome-Wallis

The carriage sidings were at the country end of Exeter Central, on the same level as the station, but the main line drops sharply to join the Paddington to Penzance main line at St Davids, where there is the famous phenomenon of trains setting out for London (and once upon a time for Plymouth) in opposite directions. In Great Western days all Southern trains had to stop at St Davids by agreement, and the tradition persisted in the 1950s, so that only one regular Southern Region passenger train passed through without stopping. This was scheduled to happen at $05.08\frac{1}{2}$, the train being the Ilfracombe portion of the 01.15 Waterloo newspapers.

The line between the two stations at Exeter has a gradient of 1 in 37. For most of the 1950s a number of 0-6-2T engines of Class E1/R, originally designed by Stroudley for the London, Brighton & South Coast Railway, were stationed at Exmouth Junction for banking Southern trains out of St Davids, and had been so employed since 1938. When on duty they waited on a spur at the Bristol end of St Davids station. Heavier passenger trains, of 11 coaches or more, usually required a pair of bankers, while some freights, especially the ballast trains from Meldon, had two rear-end bankers and a pilot engine assisting in front. There was no intermediate

Above: *Class E1/R No 32135 has just buffered up to the observation car of the 'Devon Belle', 12.00 Ilfracombe to Waterloo, at Exeter St Davids on 28 August 1954. At Exeter Central the banker will be uncoupled, the train engine, No 34050* Royal Observer Corps *will be replaced by a 'Merchant Navy', and more Pullman cars will be added at the front.* R. C. Riley

Below: *With at least one more engine pushing at the back, Class M7 No 30023 and a Maunsell 2-6-0 start the climb from Exeter St Davids to Central with an up ballast train in June 1958. The train is on the down through line for Western Region traffic.* Neil Brayshaw

Above: *In 1959 the banking of Southern trains up the 1 in 37 gradient from Exeter St Davids to Central was taken over by Class Z 0-8-0Ts. Nos 30952 and 30957 are seen on the up through and up platform roads at Exeter Central in August 1959, both carrying the disc headcode for Exeter bank engines.* Horace H. Bleads

Below: *On Easter Monday 1960 No 34058* Sir Frederick Pile, *assisted by a Class Z in the rear, climbs away from Exeter St Davids past Exeter West starter signal with the 07.26 Plymouth (North Road) to Exeter Central. Exeter West signalbox, on the Western Region main line, can be seen behind the bank engine. The usual West of England line headcode, here carried by No 34058, in fact denoted Waterloo or Nine Elms to Plymouth, and trains to Ilfracombe or Padstow carried different headcodes west of Exeter Central.* J. C. Beckett

Left: *Class 700 0-6-0 No 30327 is piloted from Exeter St Davids by Class Z No 30955 with an up freight on 15 August 1960. The train is passing between Exeter West box and South Devon carriage sidings.* Michael J. Fox

Bottom left: *For about a year the Exeter bankers were Class W 2-6-4T engines. No 31914 pushes a ballast train from Meldon across Bonhay Road bridge, nearly halfway up the incline, on 2 July 1963.* R. C. Riley

Below: *Another, presumably heavier, Meldon ballast train sets out from Exeter St Davids past South Devon carriage shed on the same day, banked by Class W Nos 31914 and 31915. At the front of the train were Standard tank No 80042 and Class N No 31858.* R. C. Riley

block post between Exeter Central B signalbox (at the west end of the station) and Exeter West box on the Paddington main line and, to save line occupation, returning bankers were frequently coupled to the front of down trains between Exeter Central and St Davids; in this way up to four engines could be seen at the head of a train coming down the bank.

Towards the end of the 1950s the 'E1/R' tanks were gradually withdrawn and their places taken by 'M7' or BR Standard tanks, and then in 1959 two Class Z 0-8-0Ts took over the banking. Three years later they in turn were replaced by two Class W 2-6-4Ts, and in the following year the Western Region, having gained control of the former Southern main line west of Salisbury, put their own 0-6-0PT engines to work on the bank.

Summer Saturdays

On Saturdays from mid-June to mid-September priority was given to traffic between London and the north coast of Devon and Cornwall, which had heavy trains with few stops east of Exeter; and between London and the seaside resorts from Lyme Regis to Exmouth, which were served by through coaches on a greatly increased scale. A succession of express trains left Waterloo from 07.30 to 12.00, and the return from the coast took place chiefly between 08.00 and 14.30, reaching Waterloo from 12.30 to 19.30. On the busiest Saturdays in July and August the overnight newspaper train from Waterloo ran in three or even four parts.

The table shows the West of England departures from Waterloo between 07.30 and 12.00 on a peak Saturday in 1956:

Waterloo to the West (peak Saturdays 1956)

Time	Destination	Refreshments	Name
07.33	Padstow, Bude	RC Okehampton	
07.38	Ilfracombe, Torrington	RC Exeter Central	
08.05	Exmouth, Sidmouth, Seaton, Lyme Regis		
08.22	Ilfracombe, Seaton	RC Exeter Central	
08.35	Ilfracombe, Torrington	RC Exeter Central	
08.57	Ilfracombe, Plymouth	RC Exeter Central	
09.00	Exmouth, Sidmouth		
10.15	Ilfracombe, Torrington	RC Exeter Central	
10.35	Padstow, Bude	RC Exeter Central	ACE
10.45	Seaton, Lyme Regis	BC Seaton	
11.00	Ilfracombe, Torrington	RC Ilfracombe	ACE
11.15	Plymouth, Padstow, Bude	RC Exeter Central	
11.45	Exmouth, Sidmouth	RC Exmouth	
12.00	Ilfracombe, Torrington	RC Ilfracombe	

RC — Restaurant car
BC — Buffet car
ACE — 'Atlantic Coast Express'

The first three stopped at Surbition and Woking to pick up only, and then ran nonstop to Salisbury. From 10.15 to 12.00 every train was first stop Salisbury, and those for Exeter reached there with not more than one further stop. The 12.00 Waterloo was the substitute for the 'Devon Belle' and each week conveyed a triple dining set, consisting of first and second class restaurant cars with a kitchen car between; in 1956 this and the 07.33 were the only down trains to go beyond Exeter intact, although later the 11.00 'ACE' did the same.

In the up direction the busiest period began at Exeter Central shortly before 11.30, with 13 long-distance departures in 3½ hours. Six trains ran from Exeter to Waterloo stopping only at Salisbury. The 'Atlantic Coast Express' swelled to four separate trains; the 10.30 Ilfracombe, 10.48 Torrington, 11.45 Bude and 11.00 Padstow. Some trains started from unusual points in order to serve the smaller stations. The 09.40 Ilfracombe to Waterloo was advertised as starting from Mortehoe & Woolacombe at 10.00. Another train introduced in 1955 ran empty from Exmouth to form the 09.45 Budleigh Salterton to Waterloo, and in later years started back at Littleham where there was a holiday camp; this train

Top right: On Saturday 13 August 1955 'King Arthur' No 30448 Sir Tristram *arrives at Salisbury with the 10.28 local train from Templecombe. The engine is already carrying the reporting number for its next working, the 12.05 Salisbury to Waterloo express, calling only at Andover Junction and Woking.* Roy Panting

Centre right: On a summer Saturday in 1957 the 08.15 Plymouth to Waterloo expanded to five separate trains: from Sidmouth, Exmouth, Seaton, Ilfracombe/Torrington, and Plymouth (in order of arrival at Waterloo). On 29 June M7 No 30374 shunts the restaurant cars which are to be added to the front of the 08.10 Ilfracombe at Exeter Central while Standard tank No 82017 appears to be backing an Exmouth branch set into the up bay. R. C. Riley

Right: Shortly afterwards 'Merchant Navy' No 35024 East Asiatic Company, *having attached a restaurant car portion to the 08.15 Plymouth, sets out for London.* R. C. Riley

combined at Seaton Junction with a through train from Seaton to Waterloo. By the time the up West of England expresses reached Salisbury it was hard to find a seat, and so a 10 or 11 coach train started there about mid-day and ran to Waterloo stopping only at Andover and Woking. On the Brighton to Plymouth service the Portsmouth portions ran as separate trains. The 12.15 from Portsmouth ran to Ilfracombe instead, and an earlier Portsmouth to Salisbury train at 09.03 was extended to Plymouth.

Many additional restaurant cars operated between Waterloo and Exeter on Summer Saturdays, but some went as far as Ilfracombe and Padstow, and down the Exmouth branch. In 1954 the down 'Atlantic Coast Express' carried a restaurant car to Padstow on Fridays, which returned on the Saturday train at 11.00, enabling lunch to be served (it would have been too late if the restaurant car had been added at Exeter). Likewise the 15.00 Waterloo on Fridays conveyed a restaurant car to Ilfracombe, though advertised only as far as Exeter; this was used in the Saturday 10.30 from Ilfracombe. Thus the Ilfracombe and Padstow sections of the up 'Atlantic Coast Express' were already complete trains when they reached Exeter on Saturdays, and were both further strengthened to 13 coaches for the run to Waterloo. In 1954 there was a restaurant car throughout on the Saturday 08.22 Waterloo to Ilfracombe which returned on a Sunday train, and a restaurant car on the 11.45 Waterloo to Exmouth, which worked to Exeter unstaffed on an evening branch train; buffet cars made return trips from Waterloo to Okehampton and Seaton.

The next year, after withdrawal of the 'Devon Belle', the triple restaurant set (the only British Railways standard triple restaurant set of 1950 vintage allocated to the Southern Region) appeared on the substitute 12.00 Waterloo, returned from Ilfracombe at 10.00 on Sundays and was normally unused until the following Saturday. The London-bound Saturday counterpart, 12.00 from

Below: Class U No 31615 hauls a heavy express from the West of England between Sturt Lane and Pirbright junctions on Saturday 10 September 1960. The engine, which must have taken over after a failure, was allocated to Guildford shed and is carrying Guildford duty number 162. The reporting number (271) belonged that year to the 08.10 Ilfracombe to Waterloo, and at the top of the number board in chalk can just be seen the figures '12.25', which was the Ilfracombe train's departure time at Salisbury where the number board was normally affixed. Derek Cross

Right: 'West Country' No 34094 Mortehoe *about to pass Vauxhall with the 11.15 Waterloo to Plymouth, Padstow and Bude on 20 June 1959, the first Saturday of the summer service. 440 is the train reporting number; the disc headcode denotes the Waterloo to West of England line; and the number 19 on the lower disc is the engine duty number and shows that this turn was the responsibility of Nine Elms shed.* P. H. Groom

Below right: Even empty trains from Clapham Yard carried reporting numbers on summer Saturdays. Shortly after 10.00 on 8 September 1962, the number 237 is hung on the bunker of Class M7 No 30035 (left) before coupling up to the stock of the 11.15 Waterloo to Plymouth, Padstow and Bude, while 'M7' No 30245 (centre) is ready to leave with the 13 coaches of the 11.00 'Atlantic Coast Express' for Ilfracombe and Torrington. So as not to occupy the main line more than necessary at a busy time, these empty trains ran through the carriage washing plant (not switched on) and joined the up through line at West London Junction instead of Clapham Junction. Author

Ilfracombe, conveyed the restaurant car off the Friday 15.00 Waterloo. The Saturday 11.00 Padstow to Waterloo had a restaurant car thoughout only at the beginning and end of the season; at peak weekends the Friday 'ACE' took the restaurant car to Ilfracombe instead, to return at 10.30 the next day, while the Saturday 11.00 Padstow had its restaurant car attached at Okehampton (still in time for lunch at 13.11), having worked down on the 07.33 Waterloo that morning. Also in 1955 a buffet car was introduced on the Saturday 09.10 Exmouth to Waterloo, working down from Exeter unstaffed in the first branch train of the day.

Trains to Waterloo on summer Saturdays carried identification numbers, from 200 upwards, attached to the smokebox door. At first the numbers were allocated week by week according to the amount of trains running, but from 1954 each train had the same number through the season. Such numbers were also used on Sunday evenings and on an ad hoc basis at other busy times, such as bank holidays, and in the summer of 1959 a similar scheme came into use for down Saturday trains, with numbers beginning at 400.

During the week the reporting numbers for up West of England trains were despatched to Salisbury, where each train had to have its number affixed. One of the main purposes was to help the operating staff at the approaches to Waterloo, and so every train on the up main line, including empty stock from Clapham Yard, and any milk or parcels trains that were running, was given a number in the order of its booked arrival at the terminus.

To relieve congestion at Clapham Yard, the coaches for some of the Saturday extras from Waterloo were stabled outside London, at such places as Esher, Teddington and Barnes, either on a more or less permanent basis or being taken there a day or two beforehand. Most of these sets were for use on the Bournemouth line, but the one kept at Barnes from Monday onwards formed the 09.00 Waterloo to Exmouth on Saturdays. The largest group of steam carriage sidings in the London suburbs, however, was at Walton-on-Thames, which provided the stock for four of the Saturday West of England departures from Waterloo. The following table shows the arrangements for 1954:

Walton-Waterloo ecs Workings (1954)

ecs dep Walton	ecs arr Waterloo	Train
06.30	07.03	07.33 Padstow
06.42	07.10	08.05 Exmouth
07.24	07.54	08.22 Ilfracombe
09.05	09.36	10.15 Ilfracombe

Below: *A regular Saturday turn for a Nine Elms Standard Class 5MT in summer 1963 was on the 00.45 from Waterloo as far as Exeter Central, returning on the 09.10 Torrington due into Waterloo at 14.37. No 73112 has just passed Farnborough with the up train one afternoon in July.* Brian Haresnape

These empty trains would usually be hauled by an 'M7' or 'H16' tank engine, an 'S15' 4-6-0 or a 'U' class 2-6-0, the engines being provided by Feltham and Guildford sheds. On the Saturday afternoon some trains of empty stock were worked down to Walton after arrival at Waterloo, travelling the long way round via Staines and Weybridge in order to be able to back into the sidings on the up side without blocking the main lines. Some had restaurant cars, which were either removed at Clapham Yard en route, or picked up and taken to Clapham by a van train on Sunday afternoon, and then taken down to Walton on the Friday for marshalling into the correct trains.

On a summer Saturday there was a great deal of turning round of stock in the platforms at Waterloo to form departures. Even so, this only happened to a minority of West of England trains, these being (in the morning) the 10.45 to Seaton and 11.45 to Exmouth, which were formed from the arrivals at 10.08 and 11.08 respectively. In the afternoon, with an almost incessant stream of arrivals, no less a train than the 15.00 Plymouth used the stock of the 14.08 arrival from Ilfracombe, while a train from Bournemouth West formed the 17.00 to Yeovil.

Bulleid Pacifics handled most of the Saturday extras in the 1950s, but smaller engines were not uncommon, sometimes working between Waterloo and Salisbury only, sometimes going through to Exeter. 'King Arthurs' had some regular turns, particularly on the early departures from Waterloo, but from 1956 onwards they were gradually replaced by Standard Class 5 4-6-0s. On the busier Saturdays, Nine Elms shed received assistance from Feltham, one of the principal freight sheds in the London area with a large allocation of 'S15s'; these were frequently seen on express passenger duty, notably on Southampton boat trains, but they even appeared on sections of the 'Atlantic Coast Express'. Feltham was also given official express duties of its own in some years, for example in 1957 and 1958 for an 'S15' from Salisbury to Waterloo non-stop on the 09.25 from Sidmouth. More rarely an 'H15' 4-6-0 or a 'Schools' 4-4-0 might be seen on a West of England express, and in the early 1950s even a 'Remembrance' 4-6-0. Apart from Nine Elms and Exmouth Junction, various turns on the extra holiday trains were worked by Salisbury shed. For instance, a Salisbury Pacific hauled the 06.45 semi-fast train each weekday to Waterloo: on Mondays to Fridays it returned on the 11.54 semi-fast from Waterloo, but on Saturdays it was used for a midday departure for the West of England, leaving the 11.54 to be worked by a Nine Elms 'H15'.

Most engines ran unchanged between Waterloo and Exeter, although several of the Saturday trains changed engines at Salisbury. Some light Pacifics ran through between Salisbury and Plymouth or Ilfracombe, not only

Below: A Feltham engine on a Feltham passenger turn. On Saturday 5 August 1961 Class S15 No 30498 works duty No 103, the 14.47 Salisbury to Waterloo, through Berrylands. This train called at all stations to Woking, then Surbiton and Waterloo. Ian J. Turnbull

on the Brighton or Portsmouth trains (the 09.50 Plymouth to Portsmouth was for some years hauled by the same engine throughout), but also on Waterloo trains. One of these was originally the heavy 08.54 or 08.57 Waterloo to Ilfracombe and Plymouth, usually 13 coaches; but on two Saturdays in 1955 the light Pacific stalled on the climb from Seaton Junction (where the train had a booked stop) to Honiton tunnel, after which the engine rosters were changed, and the Nine Elms 'Merchant Navy' hauled the train through to Exeter instead of coming off at Salisbury.

On Sidmouth/Exmouth trains the main line engine was removed at Sidmouth Junction and usually ran light between there and Exmouth Junction shed. The engine of the 10.45 Waterloo to Seaton was generally put on the front of the 14.08 Axminster stopper as pilot from Seaton Junction and reached Exeter that way. A similar arrangement in the opposite direction in 1953 and 1954 provided the express engine for an afternoon train to Waterloo from Seaton Junction; later the Seaton coaches were attached to another train.

On the Lyme Regis branch the Saturday loads of through Waterloo coaches were too heavy for a single engine. The fresh engine, coming to take over the branch for the next week, travelled up early from Exmouth Junction and the two worked together. Through trains were reintroduced in 1950, and at first there was one in each direction. The engines went down from Axminster with the usual two-coach branch set, then made a return trip with the branch set coupled to through Waterloo coaches, leaving Lyme Regis at 09.00 and returning with coaches off the through train which left Waterloo at varying times around 07.45 (later 08.05). Both engines went back to Axminster with the branch set, after which the retiring engine left for its home shed.

From 1953 onwards the 10.45 Waterloo to Seaton, instead of detaching coaches at Seaton Junction, carried a

Above: *Plenty to see at Salisbury on Saturday 29 July 1961. Feltham 'S15' No 30506 has terminated in Platform 4 with the 09.25 stopping train from Woking, whose coaches are out of the picture to the right. The S15's return working will be the 14.47 to Waterloo (see page 57). Behind No 30506, the 09.27 Portsmouth Harbour to Cardiff (train number VO7) has changed engines in Platform 3 and No 4951* Pendeford Hall *is ready to depart.* Roy Panting

Top right: *Seaton Junction on Saturday 30 July 1960. Class S15 No 30841 has just coupled up as pilot to sister engine No 30845 on the 14.08 Axminster to Exeter Central stopping train in the down platform. The reason for the double-heading was almost certainly to save a light engine working on a busy day. In the down siding is 'West Country' No 34030* Watersmeet, *which has probably come off the 10.45 Waterloo-Seaton half an hour earlier, and which did subsequently run light to Exmouth Junction shed.* R. A. Lumber

Centre right: *The Saturday 09.00 through coaches to Waterloo leave Lyme Regis on 26 July 1958 behind Nos 30582 and 30583.* R. C. Riley

Bottom right: *On Saturday 27 June 1959 a return holiday special ran from Lyme Regis to Oldham. The six London Midland Region coaches were brought to Lyme Regis on the regular 10.35 from Axminster, seen shortly after departure double-headed by Nos 30583 and 30582.* S. C. Nash

rear portion of four or five coaches for Lyme Regis, and so the two branch engines made a further round trip together, this time without the branch set. The same coaches formed the 14.35 from Lyme Regis, which was combined at Axminster with the 14.35 Seaton to Waterloo. Subsequently the Lyme Regis departure was changed to 15.05, and the through coaches were attached to the 12.45 Torrington to Waterloo.

On the Seaton branch also two engines were present to handle the Saturday traffic. In 1949 there were two sets of through Waterloo coaches in each direction, the up trains

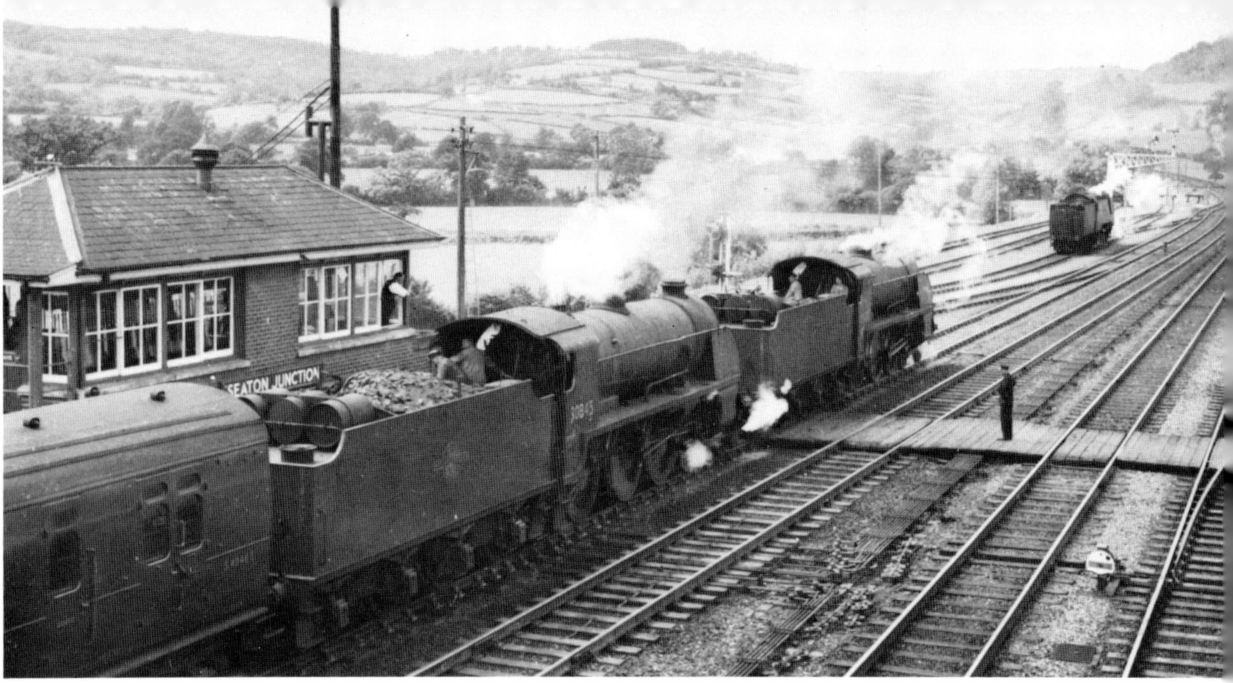
SEATON JUNCTION

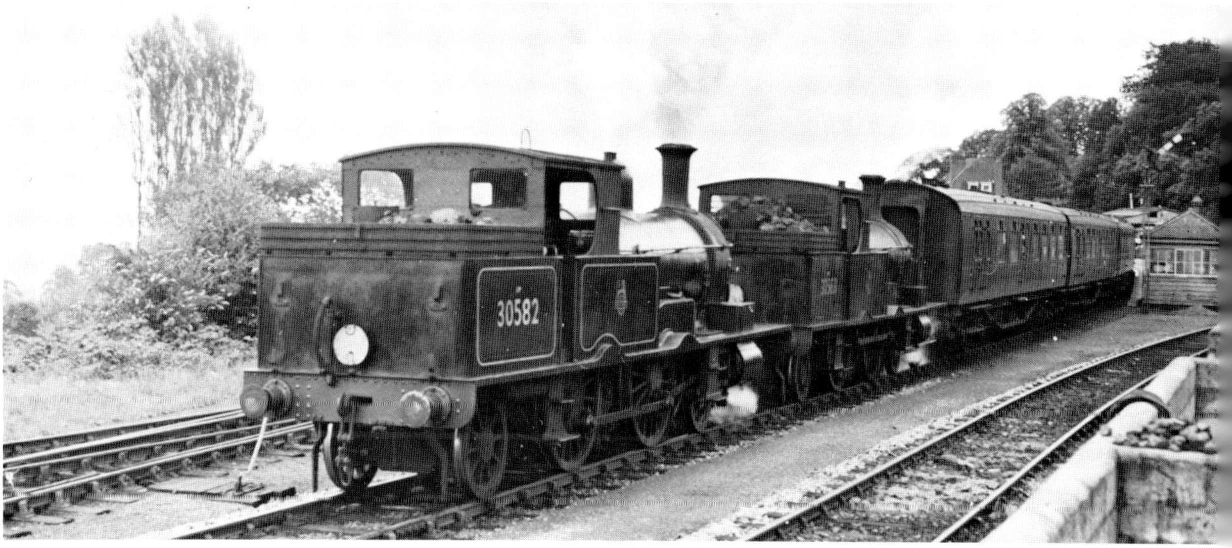
30582

30583

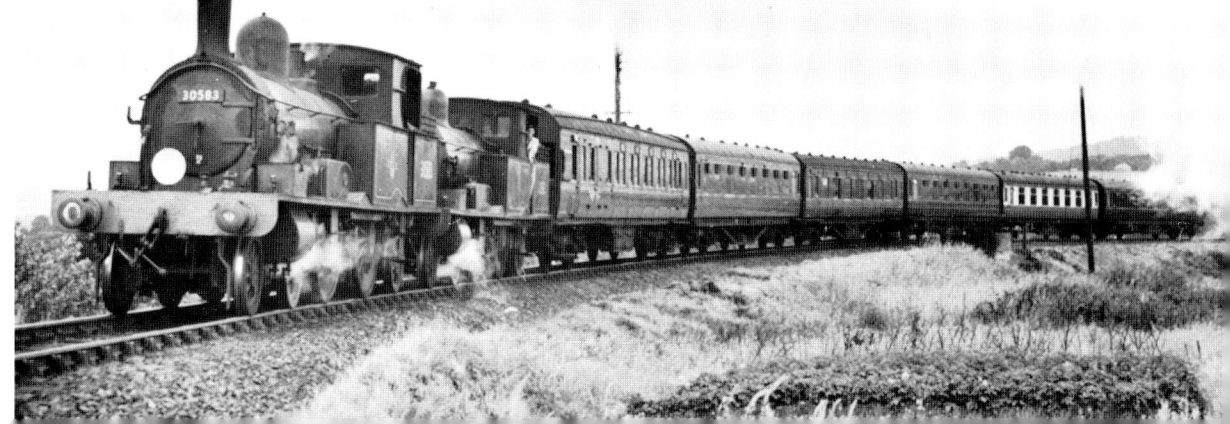

leaving Seaton at 09.00 and 10.10. The first of these consisted of seven Waterloo coaches plus the two-coach branch set, and needed double-heading to Seaton Junction, where it joined a train from Exeter. The fresh Class 0415 tank, on its way from Exmouth Junction shed to the Lyme Regis branch, was rostered to assist the 'M7' on the 09.00 from Seaton to Seaton Junction, return light engine, and then on its own hauled the 10.10 from Seaton to Seaton Junction. The 10.10 was a shorter train which combined on reaching the main line with a train from Exmouth. The '0415' then proceeded to Axminster.

By 1951, with through coaches operating between Waterloo and Lyme Regis, both Class 0415 engines were required on their own branch on Saturday mornings, and the 09.00 train departed from Seaton with two 'M7' tanks. The retiring 'M7' left for Exmouth Junction after working the 10.10 from Seaton and for the rest of the day there was only one engine on the Seaton branch. During a Saturday afternoon, however, the timetable provided two consecutive departures from Seaton Junction to Seaton without a balancing working. For three seasons, therefore, the '0415' on its way *from* Axminster to Exmouth Junction was used for a return trip on the Seaton branch, and later continued to Exeter as pilot (usually to a 'King Arthur' or 'S15' 4-6-0) on the mid-day stopping train from Salisbury.

From 1953, as we have seen, both Lyme Regis engines were busy on their own branch on Saturday afternoons, and by 1955 there was an additional afternoon through train from Seaton to Waterloo, and the 08.22 Waterloo to Ilfracombe conveyed a Seaton portion. The 09.00 Seaton to Waterloo was by then shorter, but there were several instances of two trains running successively in the same direction, and both 'M7s' stayed on the branch until mid-afternoon. In 1955 the 09.00 Seaton consisted of two or three through coaches and the push-and-pull set, and combined at Seaton Junction with the 08.30 Exeter Central and at Axminster with the 09.00 Lyme Regis. The 10.20 Seaton ran nonstop to Seaton Junction and combined with the 09.45 Budleigh Salterton to Waterloo. Then came two down trains in quick succession: two coaches off the 08.05 Waterloo to Exmouth worked with the push-and-pull set, followed by a three- or four-coach portion off the 08.22 Waterloo to Ilfracombe. This brought both 'M7s' to the Seaton end, whereupon they double-headed the 12.05 branch train back to the Junction, and one made a further round trip with loads of up to six coaches on the 10.45 Waterloo and the 14.35 Seaton. The 14.35 was formed of the stock of both the 08.05 and 08.22 Waterloo, plus the buffet car off the 10.45. This buffet car, introduced in 1954, was marshalled at the rear of the Seaton portion of the 10.45 Waterloo so that it could easily be transferred; since the turn-round was only 30 minutes it could be removed at Seaton Junction if the 10.45 was running late.

At first there were two summer Saturday trains from Waterloo to Exmouth and Sidmouth, and in 1952 a third was introduced. In 1953 the first train, 08.05 Waterloo, reached Sidmouth Junction with four coaches for Exmouth and three for Sidmouth, having already

detached portions for Seaton and Lyme Regis. It was hauled by two tank engines to Tipton St John, where it divided and one engine took each portion. The next train left Waterloo at 09.00 with the Sidmouth portion in front (until 1956), so that by the time it reached Tipton St John, having reversed at Sidmouth Junction, the seven Exmouth coaches were in front and could depart first. Two engines double-headed from Sidmouth Junction to Exmouth, and another backed on to the Sidmouth coaches at Tipton St John. One engine returned light from Exmouth to Tipton in time for the 11.45 Waterloo, which had started from Waterloo with eight coaches for Exmouth in front and four for Sidmouth at the back. This train was also double-headed from Sidmouth Junction to Tipton St John, where the leading engine came off and the other engine took the Sidmouth coaches single-handed. The second portion was then double-headed to Exmouth.

For returning holidaymakers there was one departure each from Sidmouth and Exmouth on a Saturday morning in 1951, but by 1956 there was a total of three trains in the morning and two in the afternoon. In that year three main line engines coupled together left Exmouth Junction shed at 09.20 to work the London trains from Sidmouth Junction. The first two were complete trains, the 09.25 Sidmouth and the 09.15 buffet car train from Exmouth, both of which were double-headed to Sidmouth Junction, and these were followed by the 09.45 Budleigh Salterton. After the arrival of these trains and one local service, by about 10.30 on a Saturday morning there was a regular gathering at Sidmouth Junction of six tank engines. The afternoon up trains were the 13.45 Exmouth, which combined with the return Seaton buffet car train, and the 14.20 Sidmouth, which was attached to the 11.35 Plymouth Friary to Waterloo at Sidmouth Junction.

On the Exeter to Exmouth branch there was only one through Saturday train. The 09.22, later 09.18, Exmouth to Exeter ran unadvertised as a through train to Manchester, the Southern Region timetable showing it as a train from Exmouth to Exeter Central, and the Western Region as a train from Exeter St Davids to Manchester. Even in its working timetable the Southern Region showed it as terminating at Exeter St Davids, but with a mysterious departure from that station at 10.04. The stock, usually 10 LMR coaches, reached Exmouth on the Monday evening and was stabled there for the rest of the week. On Saturday morning it left in two parts: three or four coaches, together with a regular branch set, formed the 08.21 Exmouth to Exeter Central, and when the main train of six or seven coaches, hauled by a branch tank engine, reached Exeter Central, the other coaches were added. A Western Region 4-6-0, usually a 'Hall', came up from St Davids to Central to take the train forward via Taunton and Bristol.

For a single season, in 1963, there was a corresponding down service, an overnight train from Manchester which was scheduled to terminate at Exmouth at 06.20 on a Saturday. In the late 1950s, for the benefit of passengers arriving at Exeter overnight from the Midlands and North, a transfer train of fish and parcels at 05.00 from

St Davids to Central was advertised as carrying passengers on the peak holiday Saturdays, and connected at Exeter Central with a special train running nonstop to Exmouth.

With the number of expresses running on a summer Saturday, local passenger trains were a problem to operate. Between Basingstoke and Salisbury there was nowhere a stopping train could be overtaken except Andover Junction in the up direction only, while between Salisbury and Exeter Central the only stations with platform loops were Yeovil Junction and Seaton Junction. When expresses ran late they were often delayed by stopping trains on stretches where they could not overtake; local trains in their turn would be late starting; or held, say, at Seaton Junction waiting for expresses to pass.

Virtually the full programme of stopping trains was run on summer Saturdays, with some alterations. For example, the normal 10.54 Waterloo to Salisbury started at Woking, and ran nonstop between Andover and Salisbury in order to keep out of the way of the 11.45 Waterloo to Exmouth; a 'U' class 2-6-0 from Guildford

shed replaced the usual Eastleigh 'Lord Nelson'. West of Salisbury the midday trains suffered most. In 1956 the 12.56 stopper to Exeter was timed to wait 40 minutes at Yeovil Junction and 19 minutes at Seaton Junction. Three trains were booked to overtake it at Yeovil Junction, including one which stopped there. In the other direction the weekday 13.10 Exeter Central to Salisbury was terminated at Yeovil Town; one express was booked to overtake at Seaton Junction, which cost 11 minutes, while at Chard Junction, where there was no platform loop, the local train was to be shunted for 36 minutes to allow past the Bude and Padstow sections of the 'Atlantic Coast Express' and the 12.00 Ilfracombe. After a scheduled wait of 21 minutes the same coaches returned from Yeovil Town to Yeovil Junction with a different engine and continued as a stopping train to Salisbury. During this train's absence the 11.35 Plymouth to Waterloo was booked to call at Yeovil Junction, which would have been impossible if the local train had remained there because the up bay was being used by the Yeovil Town push-and-pull train. The problem did not arise on other days because the 13.10 Exeter, with an uninterrupted passage, was timed to reach Salisbury well ahead of the Plymouth express.

Although holiday traffic had begun to fall off by the end of the 1950s, two interesting services were introduced in the summer of 1960. One was a through Saturday train between Cleethorpes and Exmouth and Sidmouth via the Somerset & Dorset line and Templecombe. In previous

Below: *After a booked 52 minute wait at Seaton Junction (during which the 11.45 Waterloo to Ifracombe went through), Standard Class 5MT No 73030, then shedded at Plymouth (Laira), restarts the 13.45 Yeovil Junction to Exeter Central stopping train on Saturday 8 August 1964. No 34015* Exmouth *shunts milk tanks in the down sidings.* W. L. Underhay

Top left: *The 10.37 stopping train to Templecombe (public timetable) or Salisbury (working timetable) sets out from Exeter Central on Saturday 20 August 1960, formed of 'King Arthur' No 30799* Sir Ironside *hauling three BR corridors.* Michael J. Fox

Left: *The 10.37 from Exeter Central was one of the stopping trains that suffered from the Saturday holiday traffic. It was booked to wait 13 minutes at Seaton Junction to allow the 09.10 Torrington to Waterloo express to pass, and reached Templecombe at 12.38 where according to the public timetable it terminated. In fact the train was shunted there for 36 minutes while two or three more Waterloo trains went by, and then continued to Salisbury. The picture shows Class S15 No 30827 leaving Crewkerne with the 10.37 Exeter Central on 26 July 1958; in the down direction both 'boards' are off for what should be — if on time — the 09.03 Portsmouth to Plymouth taking a run at Hewish incline.* R. C. Riley

Bottom left: *'Merchant Navy' class No 35029* Ellerman Lines *waits to leave Surbiton with the Okehampton Car-Carrier train on Saturday 9 July 1960, during its first season.* Alan Dixon

Above: *The 08.03 Surbiton to Okehampton Car-Carrier train arrives at Exeter Central on Saturday 20 August 1960. Here 'Merchant Navy' No 35001* Channel Packet *will be replaced, probably by a Light Pacific.* M. J. Fox

summers there had been a train between Cleethorpes and Bournemouth, but this was the first time a regular train had used this route to reach the Devonshire coast since 1939. On this train, which ran for three seasons until the Somerset & Dorset was closed as a through route, a Class 7F 2-8-0 sometimes handed over to a Class N 2-6-0 at Templecombe. The other new train was the Saturday car-carrier between Surbiton and Okehampton, which ran

for five seasons, operating for a time on Fridays and Sundays as well. There was one set of vehicles, originally seven covered vans and three passenger coaches, but another van was added in 1961, giving a capacity of 24 motor cars; the train made the round trip in the day, leaving Surbiton at 08.03 and Okehampton at 15.55. From 1961 a restaurant car was included (packed meals had been provided during the first season). 'Merchant Navy' Pacifics generally hauled the train between Surbiton and Exeter Central, stopping for water at Salisbury.

A Portrait of 1953

Saturday 8 August was one of the busiest days of 1953 on the railways. On that day, 1,050 passengers reached Ilfracombe from London alone, and probably well over twice as many departed, for the corresponding figure of arrivals a fortnight earlier had been 2,636. The tables overleaf show details of the trains in each direction on the Waterloo-Salisbury-Exeter line. The day had got off to a very bad start at Waterloo, as the 06.55 electric train to Alton and Portsmouth had failed on the down through line outside the terminus, just before the beginning of the rush of departures which was to last all morning. There were more delays to down trains beyond Salisbury, to which Honiton bank no doubt contributed. The 13-coach 11.45 Waterloo to Exmouth and Sidmouth was hauled all the way to Sidmouth Junction by an 'H15'. This engine did reasonably well as far as Salisbury and made a firm start from that city after taking water. But the 'Devon Belle' and following expresses up to and including the 13.00 Waterloo were between 30 and 60 minutes late at Exeter, and it is probable that they had been held up by the Exmouth train. The 11.45 was formed of the stock of the popular 07.30 from Exeter

Above: *On Saturday 15 August 1953 'Lord Nelson' class
No 30851* Sir Francis Drake *(of Eastleigh shed) was put on the
13.05 Waterloo to Exeter Central (booked for a Salisbury
engine). The 'Lord Nelson' failed at Basingstoke and was
replaced by 'Remembrance' class No 32327* Trevithick, *here
seen just after departure. At the time the whole 'Remembrance'
class was shedded at Basingstoke and was almost entirely
confined to semi-fast and slow services, but on this day
No 32327 worked right through to Exeter.* C. Hogg

Central, the only train for which it was thought necessary
to put a note in the working timetable, 'Load limited to 13
bogie vehicles', although in fact no train of more than 13
coaches was permitted at Waterloo as it would have been
too long for any of the platforms.

The engine rostered for the 11.45 was officially Nine
Elms duty No 10, but by that time on a peak summer
Saturday most of the best of Nine Elms shed's
locomotives would have been used, and in practice the
engine on Salisbury duty No 430, officially booked to
return on the 13.05 Waterloo-Exeter, was frequently put
on the faster and heavier 11.45. On the day in question, as
can be seen, the booked working was adhered to,
No 34049 *Anti-Aircraft Command* having arrived on the
Salisbury train due into Waterloo at 09.20.

The problem of operating stopping passenger trains on
such a day is illustrated by two instances at Salisbury.
The departure of the 14.47 to Waterloo was held back for
16 minutes because of the late running of the 10.48
Torrington, second portion of the up 'ACE'. The third
and fourth parts of the 'ACE' were also behind time, and
the 16.15 Salisbury to Waterloo was held for the 11.45
Bude and departed 11 minutes late. It was not held for the

10.45 Padstow, which reached Salisbury 36 minutes late,
and with a nonstop run to Waterloo must soon have
caught up with the stopper and have had to follow it at
least as far as Andover.

A Nine Elms 'King Arthur' No 30455 *Sir Launcelot*,
made a round trip of 330 miles on the 08.05 Waterloo to
Exmouth (as far as Sidmouth Junction) and the 12.35
Ilfracombe (from Exeter Central), and two more 'King
Arthurs', both allocated to Salisbury, worked through
from Exeter to London during the afternoon, both on
trains booked nonstop between Salisbury and Waterloo.
Two members of the 'Battle of Britain' class journeyed
through from London to Plymouth and Ilfracombe
respectively, both resting at Salisbury by coming off their
trains there and hauling a later one westward. One of
these, No 34063 *229 Squadron*, took over the 12.15
Portsmouth from Eastleigh shed's Class T9 No 30282,
which itself subsequently replaced No 5039 *Rhuddlan
Castle* at Salisbury on a Cardiff to Portsmouth train.

Several of the semi-fast trains between Waterloo and
Salisbury were handled by 'H15s' or 'S15s'. The 13.24
from Waterloo had in 1953 a booked engine change at
Basingstoke, being taken over by the engine off the 12.42
Waterloo which had terminated there three-quarters of an
hour earlier. The Nine Elms 'Merchant Navy' which
hauled the 08.54 Waterloo as far as Salisbury returned to
base on the 12.58 train, leaving the main line at
Wimbledon to reach Waterloo via East Putney and
thereby terminating one minute later than the 10.30
Ilfracombe which followed it. The 11.27 Woking, whose
path out of Waterloo was occupied on a summer
Saturday by an express for Swanage, reached Salisbury
as booked behind a Class U from Guildford shed.

Saturday 8 August 1953: Waterloo-Salisbury-Exeter

Train	To Salisbury	From Salisbury	West of Exeter	Load	Surbiton	Northam Jct	Salisbury	Exeter St Davids
07.33 Waterloo-Padstow		34054						
07.40 Waterloo-Ilfracombe		35012						
08.05 Waterloo-Exmouth		30455						
08.22 Waterloo-Ilfracombe	34005	34005		11	08.46/08.47* (6/7)			12.39/12.43 (26/26)
08.35 Waterloo-Ilfracombe	34065	34052		12	09.06/09.07 (13/11)			13.02/13.10 (36/36)
09.03 Portsmouth & Southsea-Plymouth	34053	34053				10.01 (6)		
08.54 Waterloo-Ilfracombe, Plymouth	35014	34013	34013[1] 34061[2]	13	09.18 (7)			
09.00 Waterloo-Sidmouth	34050			12	09.28/09.28 (10/8)			
10.15 Waterloo-Ilfracombe	34454		34051	11	10.34 (2)			
10.35 Waterloo-Padstow (ACE)	35010		31846 & 31841	13	10.51 (RT)			
10.45 Waterloo-Seaton	34063			8	11.05 (3)		12.27/12.31 (11/9)	
11.00 Waterloo-Ilfracombe (ACE)	35017	35017	34027	13	11.21 (4)		12.37/12.43 (6/5)	
11.15 Waterloo-Plymouth	35019	34065	34065	13	11.34 (2)		12.50/12.56 (8/8)	
11.27 Woking-Salisbury	31797			6			13.21/—— (7/—)	
11.45 Waterloo-Exmouth	30483	30483	34032	13	12.05 (3)		13.36/13.43 (15/16)	
12.00 Waterloo-Ilfracombe (DB)	35018†			13	12.18 (1)		13.52 (10)	
12.15 Portsmouth & Southsea-Ilfracombe	30282	34063	34063	9			14.04/14.11 (15/16)	
11.54 Waterloo-Salisbury	30503			6			14.26/—— (4/—)	
11.30 Brighton-Plymouth	34045		34026	11	12.12 (1)		14.30/14.35 (32/32)	
13.00 Waterloo-Plymouth, Ilfracombe	34055	34055	34059[1] 34015[2]	13			14.47/14.52 (8/7)	
13.05 Waterloo-Exeter Central	34049	34049		11	13.40 (18)		15.01/15.06 (11/7)	
13.24 Waterloo-Salisbury	30490/ 30487‡			10	13.59 (18)		16.35/—— (13)	
15.00 Waterloo-Plymouth, Ilfracombe	35023	35023	6319[1] 34017[2]	12	15.22 (5)		16.57/17.01 (15/12)	
15.05 Waterloo-Exeter Central	34001	34001		8	15.29 (7)		17.05/17.13 (13/13)	
15.54 Clapham Jc-Exeter milk empties	34014				16.27 (6)			
17.00 Waterloo-Exeter Central								
18.00 Waterloo-Plymouth	35024				18.31 (14)			
18.54 Waterloo-Yeovil Town	30453			10	19.43 (32)			

Actual time and minutes late at: Surbiton, Northam Jct, Salisbury, Exeter St Davids

Notes:

*=signal stop   †=Change engines Wilton South   ‡=Change engines Basingstoke   ACE='Atlantic Coast Express'   RT=right time   DB='Devon Belle'   E=early   V=van

([1]) and ([2]) indicate locos of separate Ilfracombe and Plymouth portions arriving or departing Exeter Central. Loads shown are those conveyed between Waterloo and Salisbury in each direction.

Saturday 8 August 1953: Exeter-Salisbury-Waterloo

| | | | | | Actual time and minutes late at: | | |
Train	West of Exeter	To Salisbury	From Salisbury	Load	Exeter St Davids	Salisbury	Surbiton
06.45 Salisbury-Waterloo			34049	6			09.01 (1E)
08.15 Salisbury-Waterloo			34055?	8			09.55 (2)
08.08 Yeovil Town-Waterloo			34001	6			10.47 (3)
07.30 Exeter Central-Waterloo			35023	13			11.00 (7)
07.10 Yeovil Town-Waterloo			30449	8			11.08 (8)
06.30 Exeter Central-Waterloo			34014	6+V			12.09 (6)
09.00 Seaton-Waterloo			30779	11			12.29 (10)
09.25 Sidmouth-Waterloo		34026	30452				13.33 (4)
11.55 Salisbury-Waterloo			35002				13.42 (5)
09.08 Exmouth-Waterloo		35002	34033	12		—/12.17 (—/RT)	13.50 (5)
08.10 Torrington-Waterloo		34033	35024	12		—/12.28 (—/1)	13.54 (2)
08.10 Ilfracombe-Waterloo		35024	31629	12			14.09 (10)
12.58 Andover Jct-Waterloo				13			
08.15 Plymouth-Waterloo		34006	34006	13		12.33/12.39 (RT/1E)	14.21 (11)
09.20 Torrington-Waterloo		35011	35011	10		12.43/12.50 (1E/RT)	14.26 (10)
08.05 Wadebridge-Waterloo		30453	30453	9		13.30/13.36 (9/9)	15.11 (23)
10.00 Mortehoe-Waterloo			30454	11			15.15 (21)
08.30 Padstow-Waterloo		35025	35025	13	12.05/12.10 (6/7)	13.49/13.56 (8/9)	15.19 (12)
09.50 Plymouth-Portsmouth & Southsea		34023	34023	8	12.20/12.25 (8/7)	14.18/14.23 (11/10)	
10.30 Ilfracombe-Waterloo (ACE)		35009	35009	13		14.27/14.33 (10/10)	
12.58 Salisbury-Waterloo			35014	4			15.43 (6)
10.48 Torrington-Waterloo (ACE)		30450	30450	12	12.44/12.49 (13/13)	14.55/15.00 (17/16)	
14.47 Salisbury-Waterloo			30333	6		—/15.03 (—/16)	15.30 (3)*
11.00 Plymouth-Brighton	34032	34058	34039				
11.30 Ilfracombe-Waterloo		34004	35019	12	12.55/13.00 (11/11)	15.05/15.11 (16/16)	16.30 (27)
12.00 Ilfracombe-Waterloo (DB)	34030	35007	35018†	13		15.43/15.50 (23/24)	
11.45 Bude-Waterloo (ACE)	31833	34005	34005	9		16.08 (22)	
16.15 Salisbury-Waterloo			30503	6+V		16.14/16.22 (22/24)	17.54 (34)
10.45 Padstow-Waterloo (ACE)	31836 & 31838	34054	34054	13		—/16.26 (—/11)	19.07/19.07 (19/18)
14.35 Seaton-Waterloo		34024	34024	11		16.37/16.43 (36/36)	18.19 (54)
11.35 Plymouth-Waterloo	34059		35012	11		16.57/17.05 (22/24)	18.32 (24)
12.35 Ilfracombe-Waterloo	34028		34055	12			18.45 (22)
13.45 Ilfracombe-Waterloo	34017		34053				19.16 (49)
17.15 Salisbury-Waterloo			30513	6			19.37 (15)
14.10 Ilfracombe Waterloo			35010	13			20.14 (36)
14.25 Plymouth	31845[1]/31792[2]						
14.55 Ilfracombe Waterloo	34056[1]/34035[2]						20.28 (19)
15.50 Plymouth Waterloo							
16.40 Plymouth-Eastleigh	34067						

* = Via East Putney
† = Change engines Wilton South

PART TWO

Paddington to Taunton and Exeter

This is a delightful journey, the track beyond Reading sometimes narrow and twisting, on either side seemingly endless farmland. If your train takes the Westbury and Frome avoiding lines, you pass through no large station for 90 miles. Any Londoner who believes that England is becoming an urban mass should go down this line to Taunton.

Unlike the Southern route described in Part One, the direct railway between Reading and Taunton did not emerge as a main line until the beginning of this century. Until then the expresses to Devon and Cornwall went via Bristol. The original main line of the Great Western Railway from London to Bristol, surveyed by Brunel, was completed as far as Reading between 1838 and 1840, and the Paddington terminus opened on its present site in 1854. At Reading a single-track branch was constructed to Hungerford in 1847 by the Berks & Hants Railway (the name was derived from a similar branch to Basingstoke), and the line was extended to Devizes in 1862. Further west the Wilts, Somerset & Weymouth Railway in 1848 completed a line to Westbury which branched from the Great Western main line at Thingley, near Chippenham, and this was extended by way of Frome and Yeovil to Weymouth in 1857. Further west still, the Bristol & Exeter Railway, opened in 1844, completed a branch 10 years later from its main line at Durston, through Langport and Martock to Yeovil.

At the turn of the century the Great Western Railway began the work of connecting these lines, and doubling the track where it was single, in order to create a shorter route from Paddington to the West. The first new section to be completed was from Patney & Chirton to Westbury, and in the summer of 1901 the Paddington to Weymouth expresses were able to use this route instead of travelling via Chippenham. Another section of new express track was constructed from Castle Cary, on the Weymouth line, to Langport on the Yeovil to Taunton branch. But instead of following the branch through Durston into Taunton, the new main line veered off at Athelney and took a short cut to the Bristol line at Cogload, an important junction named after a farmhouse. In the summer of 1906, five years after the diversion of the

Weymouth trains, the first through London to West of England expresses, including the 'Cornish Riviera Limited', used the new main line. Thus the Great Western Railway achieved its direct line to Devon and Cornwall, some 60 years after the first proposal for a not dissimilar route.

Throughout the 1920s the increasingly heavy West of England expresses had to slow through both Westbury and Frome. In the early 1930s the Great Western made use of a Government loan, part of a scheme for the relief of unemployment, to save time and coal by bypassing both towns. The cut-off lines were opened in 1933, and at the same period the flying junction at Cogload was constructed.

The various new sections of track were laid for express running. But the former Berks & Hants line, converted from a single-track branch, had numerous speed restrictions. These were operative in the 1950s although some of the curves have since been realigned. A West of England express had to slow to 40mph over the curve west of Reading and again leaving the Basingstoke line at Southcote Junction. There were further restrictions to 60mph or under at Midgham, Hungerford, and Crofton curve near Savernake. After the Westbury and Frome cut-off lines came into use the only other major restriction was to 60mph at Castle Cary, where the line to Weymouth branched off. All these speed restrictions applied to up and down trains.

In the course of establishing a new main line the Great Western, in common with all the other railway companies except those which became the Southern Railway, provided water troughs between the tracks for filling the tanks of steam locomotives while travelling at speed. These were placed 40-50 miles apart where the track was level. There were three sets on the portion of line under review, at Aldermaston, at Fairwood near Westbury, and at Creech before Taunton.

Now to describe the lie of the land along which the West of England expresses pass, remembering always that the line was constructed piecemeal. The first 36 miles on the Bristol main line roughly follow the Thames Valley and are virtually level. There are three well-known works

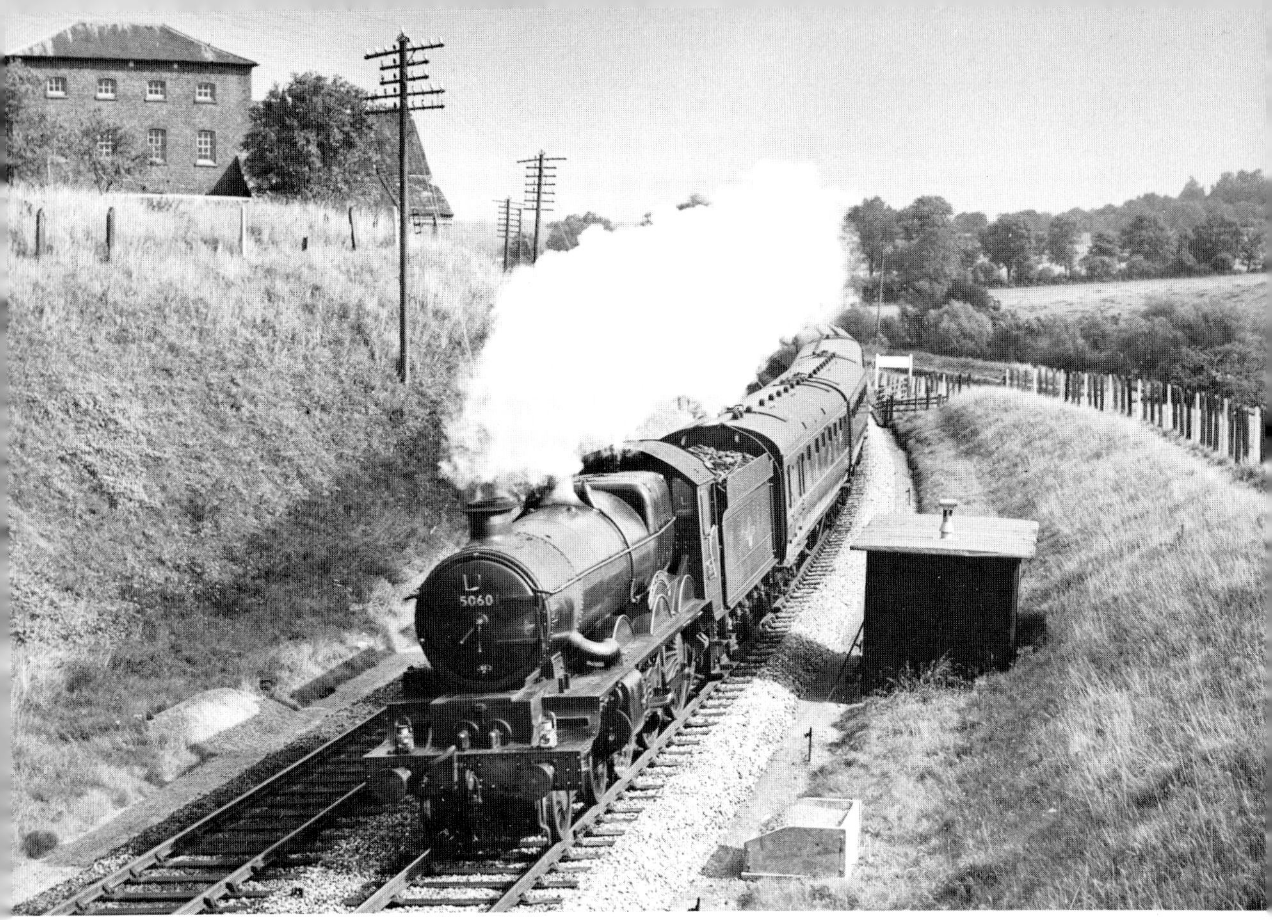
5060

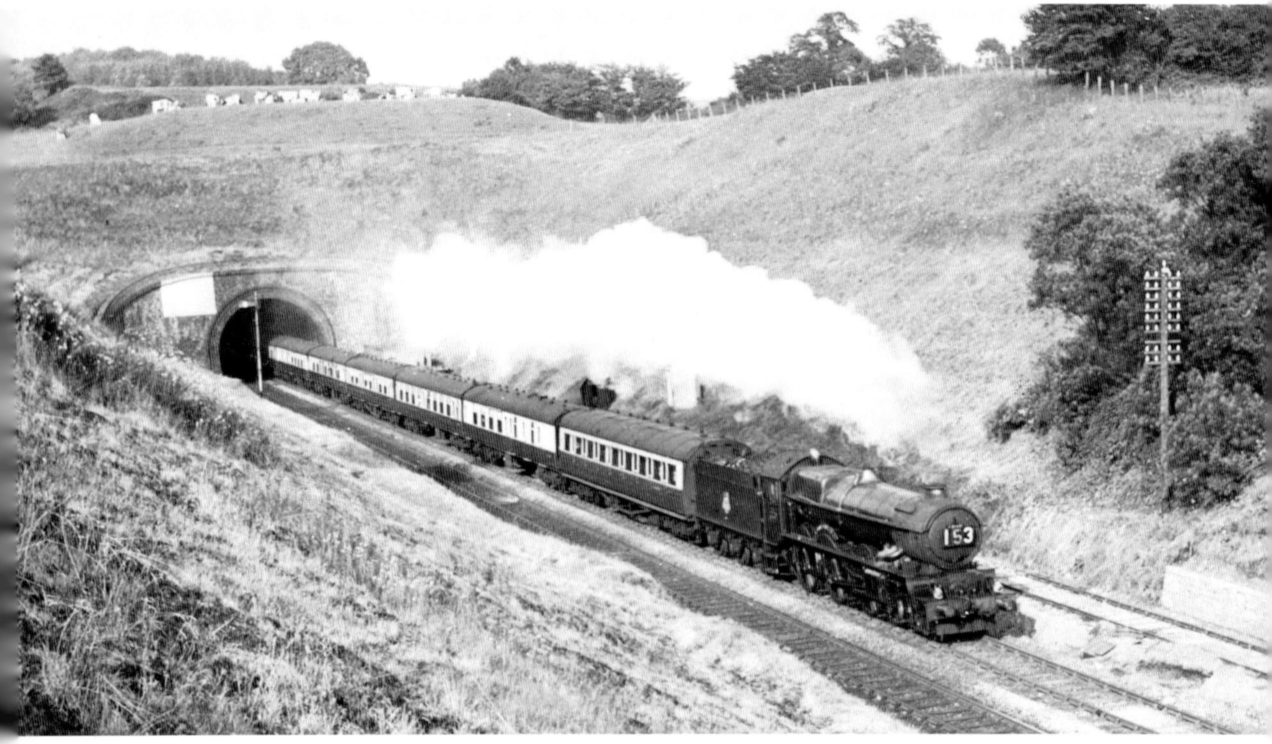
153

Above left: *Crofton curve. On 22 September 1962 'Castle' class No 5060* Earl of Berkeley *takes the curve past the pumping station and heads for Savernake with a down express.* M. Pope

Left: *The 15.30 Paddington to Penzance (the Kingswear coaches ran as a separate train on a Saturday in summer) emerges from Whiteball tunnel on 21 July 1956, hauled by No 6009* King Charles II. *The front coach, of Great Western design, is obviously additional to the regular formation of BR standard stock. The square of white paint on the tunnel brickwork is to aid the sighting of Whiteball up starter signal immediately outside.* R. C. Riley

Above: *Class 61xx tank No 6166 leaves Reading on the relief line and enters Sonning cutting with an up freight on 1 August 1953.* A. R. Carpenter

of Brunel: Wharncliffe Viaduct over the River Brent at Hanwell, the Thames bridge at Maidenhead, and Sonning cutting. At Reading the express turns due south, in the direction of Basingstoke, and bears west again after Southcote junction. From here there is a gradual climb to Savernake, mostly along the valley of the Kennet. The river and the Kennet & Avon Canal are followed as far as Hungerford, where they part company and the railway follows the canal. At Savernake the canal tunnels underneath the line, and the railway bears down the Vale of Pewsey which opens out between the Marlborough Downs and Salisbury Plain. At Patney & Chirton the main line leaves the old Devizes line at an acute angle and descends gently to Westbury. Between Westbury and Castle Cary the line tops Brewham summit, a harder climb in the eastbound direction, and thereby crosses the southern edge of the Mendip hills. After leaving the Weymouth line at Castle Cary, the main line drops gradually to sea level at Sedgemoor, a vast expanse of former marshland sometimes flooded in winter. Here the Quantock hills appear ahead, but the express meets the River Tone at Athelney and follows its course leftward into Taunton.

On a gradual ascent, the railway keeps to the Tone Vale as far as Wellington, and there, overlooked by the monument to the First Duke, begins to climb at 1 in 80 to Whiteball tunnel in order to cross the ridge of the Blackdown hills and, incidentally, the county boundary into Devon. From Whiteball summit the line descends steadily for 20 miles, following the River Culm from Cullompton to its meeting with the Exe near Stoke Canon, and then following the River Exe itself. Rail and river make junctions at Cowley Bridge, outside Exeter, the Exe with the River Yeo, and the down Western main line with the former up Southern main line from Okehampton and Barnstaple.

The line to Reading has a completely different character from the rest, and was shared with expresses to Bristol, South Wales, Cheltenham and Hereford. Of the local trains which continued west of Reading, most went to Didcot, Oxford or Swindon. Before 1955 there were irregular stopping trains between Paddington and Slough, Uxbridge or Reading, but from the summer of that year there were three trains each hour at the same times (excluding the rush hour): all stations to Slough; most stations to Reading; and semi-fast to Reading or Oxford. The rush-hour service remained much the same during the 1950s and included through trains to and from the Uxbridge, Windsor, High Wycombe (via Maidenhead) and Henley branches. Most suburban trains consisted of a Class 61xx 2-6-2T engine hauling a set of five or six non-corridor coaches, with first and second class seats (third class was renamed second in 1956). Tender engines, usually 'Halls', worked the rush-hour trains to and from Henley, Didcot and Oxford, and the fast trains terminating at Reading, with all or some corridor stock in the train.

Between Reading and Taunton the West of England expresses had a largely negative impact, in that the track had to be cleared for them but most of their passengers were travelling well past the bounds of this chapter. A number of the expresses did not stop between London and Taunton or beyond. Therefore we shall begin with the local trains, and remember the expresses later.

Stopping trains in the 1950s still followed a pattern which reflected the history of the line. There was a frequent service between Reading and Newbury or Hungerford, and of those trains which went further many took the Devizes route. Between Westbury and Castle

Cary most local trains started at Westbury itself or Bristol, and turned off towards Weymouth. There was an infrequent service between Castle Cary and Taunton, the majority of stopping trains at this end of the main line coming from Yeovil.

Regular-interval services were unknown west of Reading in the 1950s, but the service at stations between Reading and Newbury worked out very roughly at once an hour. The trains were broadly of two types, those between Reading and Newbury or Hungerford, and those which went as far as Westbury and even Bristol. The shorter journeys were mostly covered either by ex-Great Western diesel railcars or by a Class 61xx 2-6-2T engine with three or four corridor coaches or one of the suburban 'Q' sets of five non-corridors. For most of the 1950s one of the twin diesels, with an ordinary coach in the middle, was used on this section, and for some years there were regular duties both for one of these units and for a single railcar. The diesels were not infrequently out of action, and the tank engine substitues sometimes had difficulty keeping to the diesel railcar schedules and turn round times.

Some of the short-distance trains were worked by 'Halls' from Reading shed, a regular example being the 18.56 Reading to Hungerford. In the afternoons a '61xx' tank made a return trip from Reading on a stopping train as far as Savernake. A morning arrival at Reading was a train which originated at Winchester and joined the Western Region main line at Newbury; this train was

Below left: *A typical Paddington suburban train, consisting of Class 61xx tank No 6165 and six non-corridors, passes Southall shed (where No 6165 was allocated) and approaches the station on the down relief line on 13 October 1956.* C. R. L. Coles

Right: *Substituting for an ex-Great Western diesel railcar, an auto-train propelled by Class 14xx No 1444, forming the 13.21 all stations Reading General to Newbury, passes Aldermaston water troughs on 30 April 1958.* J. C. Beckett

Below: *The 11.50 from Reading General ran nonstop to Newbury and then called at all stations to Trowbridge via Devizes. Here the train is seen approaching Holt Junction from the Devizes line on 17 October 1951, behind 'Modified Hall' No 7917* North Aston Hall *of Westbury (82D) shed. The home signal behind the second coach controls the former Wilts, Somerset & Weymouth route from Thingley junction near Chippenham.* G. J. Jefferson

gradually extended until in 1958 it was starting from Totton, the other side of Southampton. For what are now known as commuters there was one through train to Paddington arriving at 09.00. This was the 07.20 Hungerford, worked by a 'Hall' class engine, which called at all stations to Theale and ran nonstop from Reading General. But there was no through train down in the evening; the best way was to use the 18.05 Paddington to Oxford to connect into the 18.56 at Reading. The 18.56 was the same engine and coaches (two corridors, five or six non-corridors and then another corridor) as the 17.20 Paddington to Reading, which crossed from the main line to the relief line after its first stop at Slough, and back to the main line outside Reading so as to terminate in Platform 4 after the 17.30 Paddington to Plymouth had passed through. The empty train was then shunted to one of the bays at the west end to form the 18.56 departure; the coaches spent the night at Hungerford and formed the next morning's 07.20 to Paddington.

The longer-distance stopping trains to and from Reading were also mainly three- or four-coach trains, usually powered by 'Hall' 4-6-0s or Class 43xx 2-6-0s from Reading or Westbury sheds. In the down direction all these trains left the main line at Patney & Chirton and ran via Devizes, terminating at Bristol, Westbury or Trowbridge. A mid-morning train from Reading ran nonstop to Newbury and then called at all stations, and an afternoon train started at Newbury instead of Reading. The up trains originated at the same places (including Bristol and Weston-super-Mare) but there were two from Westbury to Reading via Lavington, the direct route.

Between Westbury and Castle Cary there were no really small stations and many of the trains were semi-fast carrying express headlamps. Stopping trains ran on this section between Weymouth and Westbury, Chippenham or Bristol, worked mainly by 'Hall' or 'Grange' 4-6-0s

from Weymouth and Westbury sheds. Frome and Witham were connected by some of the trains on the North Somerset (Bristol-Radstock-Frome) and East Somerset (Wells-Witham) branch lines.

Beyond Castle Cary the main line to Taunton, dating from 1906, becomes largely a trunk route. In the 1950s there were a number of smaller stations, infrequently served; generally five stopping trains a day ran in each direction, most of which were push-and-pull, or auto, trains worked by Class 54xx 0-6-0PT engines. Often the train, instead of being worked push-and-pull, was hauled by a '57xx' pannier tank or one of the larger '45xx' 2-6-2T engines, and for a time the engine and coaches of the first train of the day from Taunton to Castle Cary in fact worked through from Minehead. Some trains were extended beyond Castle Cary. The first down train started from Westbury, and there was a corresponding evening working back to Westbury or Frome. A down train in the evening originated at Melksham. Between Athelney and Taunton, in either direction, the stopping trains had a choice of routes. Some took the old Yeovil branch, joined the Bristol main line at Durston and approached Cogload from the Bristol direction; others continued to Cogload on the newer cut-off line, which meant running non-stop to Taunton.

According to the public timetable two of the up stopping trains took some 20 minutes to get from Alford Halt to Castle Cary, normally a five-minute journey.

Below: *On 5 March 1960 No 4917* Crosswood Hall *awaits departure from the down bay at Newbury with the 16.36 stopping train to Westbury via Devizes. The coaches will have formed the rear portion of the 14.35 Paddington to Weston-super-Mare, detached at Newbury.* Bryan S. Jennings

What in fact happened was that the trains were shunted at Somerton to allow expresses to pass. For some years the 11.45 from Taunton was scheduled to wait 20 minutes at Somerton for the early morning express from Truro, later Penzance, to Paddington, while throughout the 1950s the 15.45 Taunton spent 15 minutes there being overtaken by the train from Penzance which later became the up 'Royal Duchy'. The public timetable ignored these long waits and became out of step with the working timetable so that, if the express was running very late, the local train could leave Somerton at once without being ahead of its advertised time. For the arrival at Castle Cary public and working timetables were brought back into harmony.

All stations which were not merely halts were served in the 1950s by local, or pick-up, goods trains, which stopped, shunted usually for up to half-an-hour, and moved on. But they did not necessarily follow the main line. For example, there was a trip from Didcot via Compton to Hungerford, and back; and one between Westbury and Ludgershall, leaving the main line at Savernake. Goods yards at Bedwyn, Savernake, Patney & Chirton and the adjoining stations were shunted in the early hours of the morning by two trains proceeding in opposite directions, the 02.15 Reading to Holt Junction and the 03.15 Bristol East Depot to Reading, both via Devizes. Places further west were served by a return trip from Westbury to Sparkford, on the Weymouth line, and a trip from Castle Cary to Durston and back.

Reading, Westbury and Taunton, and in the summer Newbury and occasionally Frome, were the only stations regularly served by West of England expresses. But the Paddington to Weymouth trains called at several of the smaller places, such as Hungerford and Savernake, Lavington and Bruton. For most of the 1950s there were two of these in each direction. The fastest was the 12.30 Paddington, which stopped only at Newbury and Lavington between Reading and Westbury. This train carried a restaurant car (at times only a buffet car) as far as Westbury. The 09.00 Weymouth to Paddington, which terminated at lunchtime, had a restaurant car throughout which returned to Weymouth on the 18.00 Paddington. The 18.00 was non-stop to Newbury, so as not to be filled with rush hour passengers to Reading, and consisted of two and sometimes three portions. The front coaches with the dining car ran to Weymouth Town. Three evenings a week in winter some of these coaches, with the addition of a luggage van, ran instead to Weymouth Quay for the night sailing to Guernsey and Jersey, and thereby formed a middle portion. The rear coaches were removed at Newbury and ran as a stopping train to Trowbridge via the Devizes line. The inward sailing from the Channel Islands in winter was in the daytime, and three times a week the 16.10 Weymouth to Paddington included coaches from the Quay. This train, like some of the other Weymouth expresses, changed engines at Westbury, and the new engine, sometimes one of Reading shed's 'Castles', added a restaurant portion to the front. The 18.00 Paddington also changed engines, and was taken down to Westbury often by a 'Castle' and occasionally even a 'King'. Otherwise it was the 'Hall' Class which

almost invariably managed the Weymouth trains. Until 1954 another train, at 11.40 from Weymouth, ran to Paddington in the summer, and had originally run all year, classed as a stopping train as far as Westbury, where it changed to express headlamps; after 1954 this train or its equivalent ran only on summer Saturdays.

There were two through trains to Paddington every morning from Wiltshire, but the earliest arrival, by the 07.15 Trowbridge, varied between 10.05 and 10.15. This train went via Devizes, calling at most stations to Newbury, where it became an express, although it did stop at Midgham as well as Reading. The return, after a full day in London, would be by one or other portion of the 18.00 Paddington, depending upon the importance of the home station. The second up train was the 08.15 Frome, which took the direct Lavington route and carried express, or Class A, headlamps although stopping a number of times before Newbury. Until 1954 this train ran through from Weymouth, departing at 06.30, on Mondays, Thursdays and Saturdays. Paddington was reached at 11.15. For some time the engine on this train could be predicted with certainty: day after day No 6994 *Baggrave Hall*, of Westbury shed, appeared, then worked through to Weymouth on the 12.30 Paddington, and back to Westbury on the evening milk train.

A train in a category of its own was the 14.35 Paddington to Weston-super-Mare via Devizes. Roofboards showing 'Paddington, Bristol and Weston-super-Mare' were generally carried on the coaches, and there was no outward sign of the unusual route. The train, usually in charge of a 'Hall', stopped before Devizes at Reading, Newbury and Savernake, and for a time also at Woodborough, only on notice being given to the guard, to set down passengers from Paddington or Reading. A rear portion was detached at Newbury and later formed a stopping train to Westbury, although not an official through coach working; in winter 1955, for example, the regular formation was eight coaches of which only the front four worked to Weston-super-Mare. There was no equivalent train in the up direction, the nearest being the afternoon stopping train from Weston-super-Mare to Reading.

The through coaches to Weymouth Quay in winter have been mentioned, but from May to September, a slightly longer period than the normal summer timetable, there was a daytime sailing in each direction between Weymouth and the Channel Islands. An impressive dining car train, usually an Old Oak Common 'Castle' and 12 coaches, left Paddington for Weymouth at different times crystallising in 1954 at 08.20, and called only at Reading (to pick up), Westbury and Yeovil. The same engine and coaches connected with the inward boat and left Weymouth at tea-time, reaching Paddington shortly after 19.30. The up train stopped at Frome instead of Westbury, for a reason which will become apparent later. These boat trains were the only regular Weymouth line trains to carry large Western Region reporting numbers on the front of the engine. Until 1950 independent boat trains ran in connection with the winter sailings too. The up boat train left Weymouth three times

a week at the same time as in summer; the outward sailing, however, was at night, and the boat train left Paddington at 21.10.

Other Weymouth expresses used the line between Westbury and Castle Cary. They were nearly all to and from Bristol, and reached Westbury by way of Bradford-on-Avon and Trowbridge. As a rule they stopped at Westbury, Frome and Castle Cary, and some also at Witham and Bruton, but one train in each direction ran nonstop between Frome and Yeovil. Around 1950 the 08.05 Bristol to Weymouth and the 12.35 back normally consisted of one of the twin diesel units, but this proved insufficient for the summer loading, and from 1952 the diesel was rostered in winter only. This working ended altogether in 1954 but it remained a return trip for the engine and coaches, of which there were usually four in winter and up to 10 in summer. Bristol Bath Road shed provided the engine, and often used a 'Castle' for the turn.

The other regular train to use this stretch of line was the through Wolverhampton to Weymouth express, which approached Westbury along the original line of the Wilts, Somerset & Weymouth Railway from Chippenham through Melksham. The train ran every weekday in the summer, but only on Saturdays in winter. Departure from Weymouth was near 10.30; the down train left Wolverhampton after 11.00 and reached Westbury in the middle of the afternoon. There was a complete set of carriage roofboards, 'Wolverhampton, Birmingham, Oxford, Swindon & Weymouth'.

Castle Cary was not a stopping point for West of England expresses, and only local trains connected it with Taunton. Between Castle Cary and Cogload the only regular passenger expresses (except on a summer Saturday) were between London and Plymouth, Cornwall or Torbay.

One of the best-known trains in the country, and one of the comparatively few named trains which still exist on the Western Region at the time of writing, travelled every day, including Sundays, along the stretch of line described in this period without making any booked stops. The

'Cornish Riviera Express' — often known as the 'Cornish Riviera Limited' — was introduced in the summer of 1904 and ran nonstop to Plymouth via Bristol. Two years later, on completion of the main line via Castle Cary, the 'Limited' began to use the shorter route, and its departure from Paddington was fixed for 65 years at 10.30. Between the wars the 'Limited', like the Southern's 'Atlantic Coast Express', ran in many portions. For most of the 1920s and 1930s there were coaches for Penzance, St Ives, Falmouth, Newquay and Plymouth, and at one time the down train in winter slipped coaches at three different points, Westbury for Weymouth, Taunton for Minehead and Ilfracombe, and Exeter for Kingsbridge.

During the 1950s the down 'Limited' consisted of three portions. Most of the train, including the dining cars, ran to Penzance; one or two coaches were detached at Plymouth, and one or more were slipped near Westbury for Weymouth. Only the Plymouth and Weymouth coaches had roofboards showing where they were going; the Penzance coaches merely bore the legend 'Cornish Riviera Express'. Most of the up train ran through from Penzance, but coaches were added to the front at Plymouth. Winter and summer there was a pathway for a relief train to run when required from Paddington to Penzance.

In June 1955 the four-hour schedule to Plymouth in the down direction was reintroduced for the first time since World War 2. The load of the down 'Limited', as far as the slipping point for Weymouth at Heywood Road junction, Westbury, might be as much as 14 coaches, but in summer 1956, when the Western Region formed all its named trains from a batch of chocolate and cream coaches, the down 'Limited' was put on a special load

Right: 'Castle' class No 7000 Viscount Portal *passes under the MSWJ line to Savernake (High Level) on 17 August 1957 and approaches Wolfhall junction signalbox with the down 'Torbay Express'. In the foreground is the spur from Grafton South Junction to Wolfhall, used by MSWJ trains travelling via Savernake (Low Level).* Kenneth Leech

Left: *The 14.35 Paddington to Weston-super-Mare took the Berks & Hants route at Reading and reached Bath via Devizes and Bradford-on-Avon. A rear portion was detached at Newbury. On 30 June 1956 the front portion consisted of BR standard coaches with 'Paddington Bristol and Weston-super-Mare' roofboards, and No 6870* Bodicote Grange *is seen hauling the train past Acton West box as Class 57xx No 9704 leaves Acton Yard with a down freight.* R. C. Riley

timing and not allowed to exceed 10 coaches; if it did, the scheduled time was increased. At first only passengers with reserved seats could join the train, but this rule was abandoned after the first summer. On days when the 10.35 relief ran, the Weymouth slip coaches were conveyed by the relief and not by the main train.

The other famous named train was the 'Torbay Express', introduced between Paddington and Kingswear in 1923. In the 1950s the whole train ran to Kingswear, leaving London at 12.00 and Kingswear at 11.25, two sets of coaches being used. Except at peak periods the basic load of the 'Torbay Express' was only seven or eight coaches, and like the 'Cornish Riviera Limited' it became chocolate and cream in 1956. The 'Torbay Express' was nonstop between Paddington and Exeter, and ran daily in the summer, but Sundays excepted in winter. For most of the 1950s, 'Castles' from Newton Abbot shed handled the train in both directions.

Roughly every two hours a West of England express passed along the direct main line. In the early 1950s the first train of the day to leave Paddington for the West by this route was the 'Limited' itself, but in summer 1953 a new train ran to Newquay and Falmouth departing at 09.30, and at the same time a train began running from these resorts to Paddington ahead of and in relief to the up 'Limited', nonstop from Plymouth. The following year the 09.30 Paddington became an all-year-round train, terminating at Plymouth during the winter, and replaced the 11.00 Paddington to Plymouth. Meanwhile in 1954 a summer-only train was introduced at 11.30 from

Paddington to Plymouth, and later extended to Penzance; the 11.30 called at Reading, Newbury and Taunton, where (for the first two summers) it was overtaken by the 'Torbay Express' which had left Paddington half-an-hour later. So on a summer morning from 1954 onwards expresses left Paddington for the Berks & Hants route to the West at 09.30, 10.30, 11.30 and 12.00.

Of the regular down expresses only the 13.30 Paddington, which became the 'Royal Duchy' in 1957, took the right-hand line at Heywood Road junction and stopped at Westbury. The 15.30, first stop Taunton, conveyed, like the 'Cornish Riviera Limited', one or more slip coaches for Weymouth. In each case the coaches were slipped at Heywood Road junction, and the main train continued on the Westbury avoiding line. The slip portion was then collected by a station pilot and attached to the rear of a Weymouth-bound train at Westbury. The slip coach off the 10.30 Paddington reached Weymouth on a stopping train from Chippenham. The 15.30 slip coach was handled with more despatch; by the time it reached Westbury the 16.25 Bristol to Weymouth express, if punctual, was already there. Attached to this train, the slip coach was on the move again in seven minutes, and reached Weymouth in an overall time of under $3\frac{1}{2}$ hours. The last daytime express, the 17.30 Paddington to Plymouth, also first stop Taunton, was named the 'Mayflower' in 1957. A prewar train to Kingswear on Fridays in the summer was revived in 1956 and left Paddington at 19.30 (later 19.25), nonstop to Taunton.

Three of the up West of England trains called at Westbury. The first of the day, the 07.15 Plymouth, reached Paddington at 12.15 after running from Westbury non-stop. The 08.30 Plymouth, which became the up 'Mayflower', did the same, but conveyed a slip coach for Reading. The next train to stop anywhere between Taunton and Reading was not until evening. The 11.00 Penzance to Paddington, which became the up 'Royal Duchy', stopped at Westbury all the year round and Newbury in the summer. Thus, with the stop made by

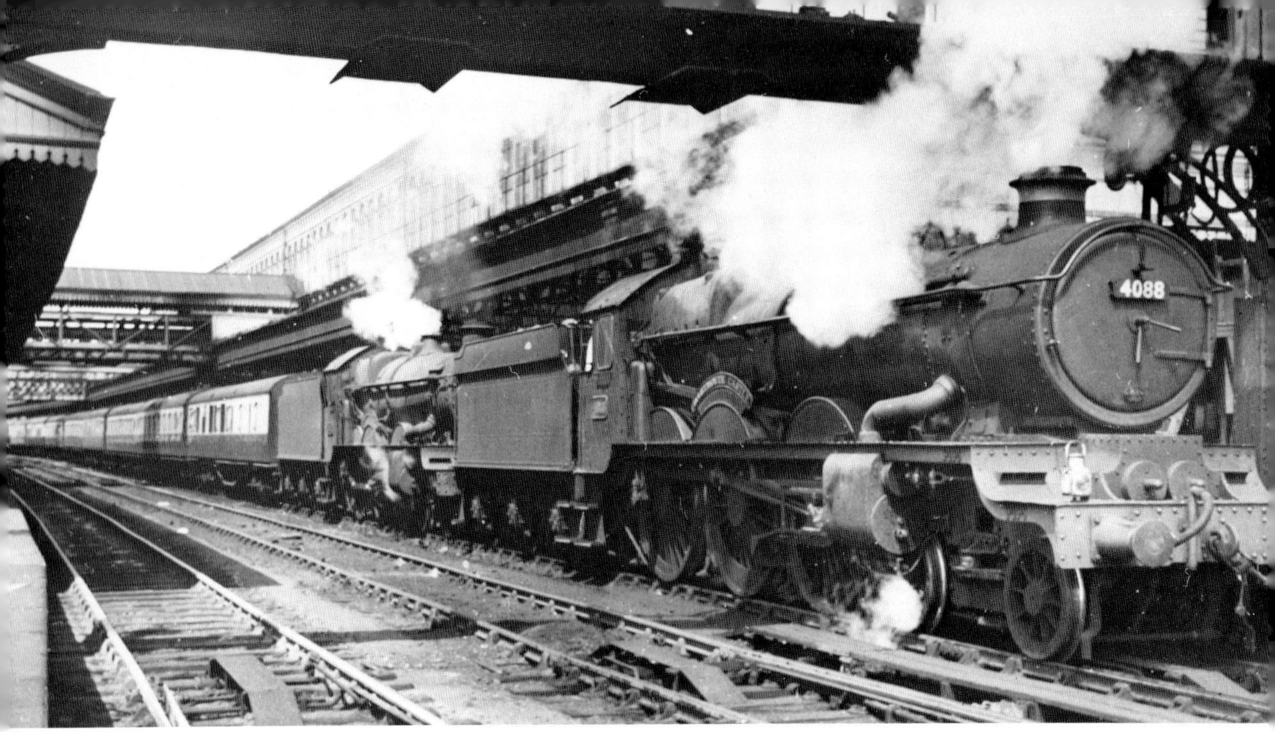
4088

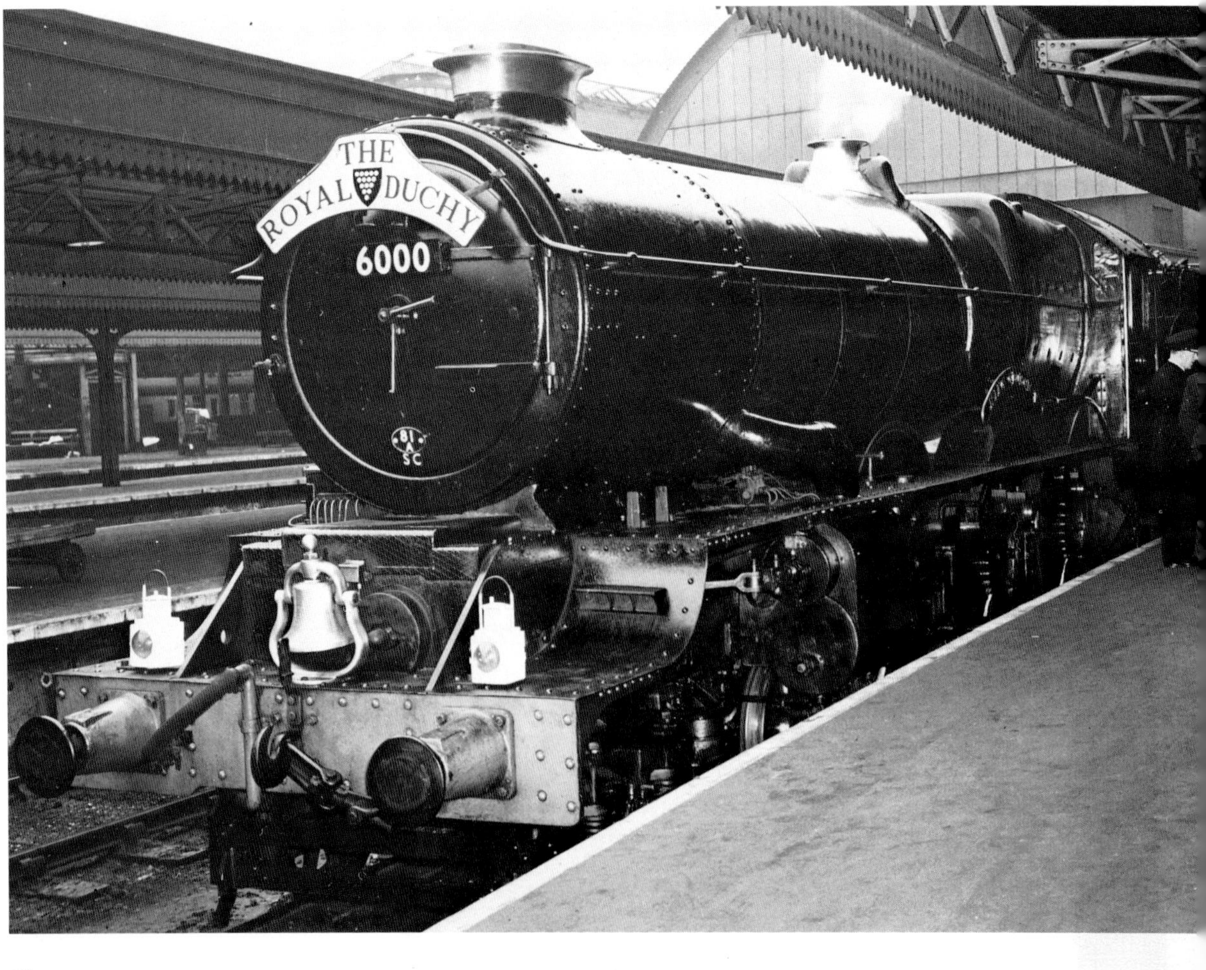
THE
ROYAL DUCHY
6000

Above left: *In the early 1950s a train left Paddington for Plymouth at 11.00, and on Mondays only was booked to convey five empty coaches for Newton Abbot at the back, which had worked up on a Sunday evening train. On 21 May 1951 the Monday load leaves Platform 1 at Exeter St Davids double-headed by Nos 4088* Dartmouth Castle *and 7032* Denbigh Castle. *A gas tank wagon occupies the down through line in the distance.*   Cecil G. Pearson

Left: *As from 28 January 1957 the 13.30 Paddington to Penzance and Kingswear was named the 'Royal Duchy'. On the inaugural run the train was hauled by No 6000* King George V, *here seen waiting to leave Platform 1 at Paddington.*   BR

Above: *On 3 July 1958 the down 'Royal Duchy', 13.30 Paddington to Penzance and Kingswear, with chocolate and cream coaches, leaves Exeter St Davids for its next stop at Newton Abbot behind No 4089* Donnington Castle. *According to the gantry on the left an up train is signalled into Platform 5, but the line is not clear beyond the station as Exeter Middle box distant is on.*   J. Scrace

the 11.30 Paddington, Newbury had a through summer-only service to and from the West.

More than half the West of England expresses in the 1950s conveyed portions to and from both Plymouth or beyond and the Torquay branch. Apart from the 'Torbay Express', restaurant cars usually worked between Paddington and Plymouth, but those on the 'Cornish Riviera Limited', and the trains which became the down and up 'Royal Duchy', went through to Penzance.

The principal overnight sleeping car trains to and from the west, and the night mail trains, ran via Bristol. However, the newspaper train to Penzance via the direct line, leaving Paddington soon after midnight, included sleeping cars but no ordinary coaches. It was not advertised in the passenger timetable until 1957, by which time it was booked to reach Taunton, its first stop, at exactly a mile a minute. At summer weekends and before bank holidays a separate train, formed only of sleeping cars, followed the newspaper train. Going east, a train of sleeping cars ran throughout the summer (from 1953) and after Easter and Whitsun.

Apart from the 'Torbay Express', all the regular West of England expresses via the direct route were through engine workings between London and Plymouth. The engine normally returned home the next day, and the crew lodged overnight. 'King' class engines from Old Oak Common (London) and Laira (Plymouth) sheds hauled most of the trains, supplemented by 'Castles', and from 1951 to 1956 by a number of 'Britannia' Pacifics which were then based at Laira or Old Oak Common. In the early 1950s one or other of the Western Region's experimental gas turbine locomotives, Nos 18000 and 18100, had periodical tours of duty on the line. For the winter service of 1956 six out-and-home workings were devised for 'King' engines (three each from Old Oak Common and Laira) to work back to their home shed within 24 hours of leaving. The return trips for the three Old Oak Common engines were all overnight, on a perishables train and a milk train from Penzance, and the sleeping car train via Bristol.

Of the special passenger trains over the line perhaps the most exciting were the often lightweight boat expresses which from time to time dashed from Plymouth Millbay to Paddington, usually in the eastbound direction and hauled by a Laira 'Castle'. They were not frequent in the 1950s, since Plymouth was no longer a regular port of call for most ocean liners, but for a time the *Liberté* and other French liners were often in too great a hurry to do more than despatch tenders to Plymouth on their way

Above: *'Modified Hall' No 6965* Thirlestaine Hall, *of Laira shed, approaches Hungerford on Sunday 8 July 1956 with the 14.45 Kensington to Plymouth milk empties.* R. C. Riley

from New York to Le Havre. Like all boat trains they were liable to be run at short notice, and a number of point-to-point schedules existed between Millbay and Paddington, depending on the weight of the train. Those for a nonstop run had the code-names Plym A, B, C and D, and the fastest was 4 hours 17 minutes, although in practice the journey was often completed in less than 4 hours.

There were a number of non-passenger express trains. Milk trains left Penzance for Kensington at 12.20 and 18.20 and came up respectively in the late evening and the middle of the night. The train of empty milk tanks to Plymouth went down in the afternoon after the 15.30 Paddington. There was enough perishables traffic for one, and later two, regular trains to leave Penzance for Paddington in the afternoon. The second was faster and was classed as a meat train. Extra trains ran when certain types of produce, such as broccoli, spring flowers and new potatoes, were in season. Two express parcels trains left London for Penzance in the evenings, both stopping to change crews at Heywood Road junction. Then there were several express goods trains which ran through the night to Penzance, Newton Abbot or Weymouth. Some, for example the 20.55 to Penzance which ran from Paddington to Taunton without a booked stop, were

hauled by the Class 47xx 2-8-0s, more often seen by night than by day.

There were engine sheds at Reading (81D), Westbury (82D) and Taunton (83B). In 1956-7 Reading had over 20 'Hall' 4-6-0s and two 'Castles'. Westbury and Taunton had a number of 'Halls' but no 'Castles'. Taunton had several 'Grange' 4-6-0s for mixed traffic work, Westbury had one, but Reading none. All three sheds, especially Reading, had a number of Class 43xx 2-6-0s, and all had '2251' 0-6-0s for local freight and some passenger work, and one or two '28xx' 2-8-0s for heavy freight. For stopping passenger trains Reading had numerous '61xx' suburban tank engines and some of the smaller postwar '94xx' class tanks; Westbury had the small '54xx' class tank engines for push-and-pull trains, and some of the larger '45xx' 2-6-2Ts; Taunton had both '45xx' and '51xx' 2-6-2Ts, and two auto-fitted '54xx' class. All three sheds had plenty of '57xx' pannier tank engines, for shunting and local freight and passenger trains.

A few years earlier, in 1950, Taunton had two 'Castles', while three of the remaining 'Star' 4-6-0s were allocated to Westbury; Reading had some of the 'Grange' class; and Westbury, instead of Class 28xx, had three of the Austerity 2-8-0s built during World War 2.

In the London area Old Oak Common (81A) was the principal shed, and the home of passenger and express goods ('47xx' class) engines, shunting engines and carriage pilots; Southall (81C) was primarily a freight and mixed traffic shed, with some local and branch passenger engines and diesel railcars; Slough (81B) had tank engines for branch line and local work.

Locomotive Allocations — July 1953

Class	Reading (81D)	Westbury (82D)	Taunton (83B)	Exeter (83C)
'Castle' 4-6-0	3			3
'Modified Hall' 4-6-0	4	4	1	1
'Hall' 4-6-0	16	6	6	2
'Grange' 4-6-0	3		3	
43xx 2-6-0	14	13	10	4
28xx 2-8-0		1	1	
2251 0-6-0	4		10	1
2301 0-6-0	1	2		
51xx 2-6-2T			5	1
61xx 2-6-2T	15			
45xx 2-6-2T		5	13	1
56xx 0-6-2T		3		
57xx 0-6-0PT	19	17	13	10
94xx 0-6-0PT	6			2
2021 0-6-0PT			1	
1366 0-6-0PT			1	
54xx 0-6-0PT		6	3	
14xx 0-4-2T	3			8
1361 0-6-0ST			1	
Ex-Cardiff Railway 0-4-0ST			1	
Ex-Powlesland & Mason 0-4-0ST	1			
AEC diesel railcar	4			

Except for the first ten miles out of Paddington the line to Taunton and Exeter via Castle Cary had lower-quadrant semaphore signals worked on the block system. The main line was also equipped with automatic train control (corresponding to the present automatic warning system in its functions), a safety device introduced by the Great Western Railway in 1906 and installed between Paddington and Reading a few years later. A ramp was placed between the rails near every distant signal, and would be struck by a shoe carried on the locomotive. When the distant signal was in the 'clear' position a bell rang in the driver's cab; when the signal was at caution a hooter sounded. The system was particularly useful in the London smogs which still came down in those days (and were not confined to central London); with a clear road trains could run at a high speed even when the signals were practically invisible.

Below: *Class 28xx 2-8-0 No 2847 passing Clink Road junction with a freight train.* Ivo Peters

Stations and Junctions

Paddington to Old Oak Common and Acton (Main Line)

Paddington station was built by Brunel and opened in 1854. By its centenary in 1954 the terminus was in two parts and had a total of 16 platforms, 12 in the Main station and the remainder in the Suburban station. At Paddington Suburban the outer platforms (Nos 13 and 16) were used by the Metropolitan Line trains to and from Hammersmith which shared one pair of tracks with the Western Region suburban trains as far as Royal Oak.

The Main station was divided into arrival and departure sections, each with its own signalbox, and the down and up main lines were then separated by a group of sidings known as Paddington Yard, so that Subway junction, nearly a mile from the terminus, was the first signalbox to control both up and down lines. In those days the stock for long-distance departures was almost without exception brought in empty, and the stock of long-distance arrivals taken out empty. Only Platforms 5 and 6 could be used for both arrival and departure of passenger trains (unless recourse was had to one of the empty carriage lines), Nos 1 to 4 being purely departure platforms and Nos 7 to 11 purely for arrivals (No 12 was and is a short parcels platform leading off Platform 11). In the 1950s the only occasion when the coaches of an arriving long-distance train were regularly scheduled to be turned round to form a departure from the same platform was on a summer Saturday and even then it happened only once in the day.

Many of the engines for main line departures from Paddington were of course provided by Old Oak Common shed, and some, especially at busy times, were used to haul to Paddington the empty coaches for an earlier departure, although the more important engines were not usually put to such work. Visiting engines from sheds outside London were serviced at Old Oak Common if there was time, but many, particularly from Worcester, Gloucester, Bristol (Bath Road) and Wolverhampton (Stafford Road) sheds, were booked to leave Paddington an hour or two after arrival, and these went to Ranelagh Bridge, a small depot with a turntable just outside Paddington on the down side.

At Old Oak Common there was not only an engine shed but a large carriage depot and sidings and a marshalling yard. Old Oak Common provided the stock for nearly all long-distance departures, and most of the empty trains were hauled to and from Paddington in the 1950s by Class 15xx, 94xx and 57xx engines. To enable empty trains to reach the departure side at Paddington from Old Oak Common carriage sidings (on the up side), the up carriage line crossed the main lines by a bridge near Old Oak Common East box and ran on the south side of the down main line. There were two up carriage lines between Subway junction and Paddington, the down main line being in the middle. Empty trains from Paddington to Old Oak Common likewise used the down carriage line which remained on the up side throughout.

A set of coaches which was due to leave London again between three and six hours after its arrival at Paddington was considered in the 1950s to have a short margin, and a special list of the trains concerned was kept at the front of the Paddington station working book. If the down carriage line was congested, the empty coaches of these trains were to run to Old Oak Common via the down main line and the overbridge (which then carried down and up lines).

Almost opposite Old Oak Common and on the down side were West London carriage sidings, which contained the stock for shorter-distance trains, particularly in the rush hours (for example, the 07.20 Hungerford to Paddington already mentioned), and for some of the holiday extras.

Paddington Yard was used mainly for suburban sets and in the early evening for instance, the coaches of the 16.34 Paddington to Banbury and the 16.48 to High Wycombe were coupled together in the Yard and drawn into Platform 4, departing successively from the same platform. A few of the local trains using the Main station were turned round in Platforms 5 or 6, and most arrivals in the Suburban station were turned round to form departures, usually with the same engine (which, being a tank engine, did not have to be turned).

On the freight side, the principal London depots or yards were at Paddington, Old Oak Common and Acton.

Above: *Class 15xx No 1504 passes Westbourne Park on the up carriage line with an empty train from Old Oak Common to Paddington on 8 May 1962. The track in the foreground is the down main and the signalbox is Portobello junction. The engine is carrying the number 5 on the buffer beam; this was one of the target numbers allotted to each Paddington carriage pilot for its tour of duty, and generally carried at busy times.*
Ian Allan Library

Below: *A down train of milk empties, having no doubt reversed out of West Ealing milk depot, departs from the up relief line at West Ealing on 17 May 1952 behind No 7029* Clun Castle. *The engine is carrying Class C (express freight) headlamps.*
C. R. L. Coles

Main-Line Departures from Paddington during the Evening Peak — Summer 1956

Departure Time	Destination	Platform	ECS from	First stop	Switched to RL at	Usual Engine	Booked formation	Remarks
16.30	Reading General	2	WL	West Drayton	W Drayton East	'Hall' (81D)	10 (all but 3 non-corridor)	
16.34	Banbury	4	Yard	Gerrards Cross	Subway junction		5	
16.38	Worcester	3	OOC	Reading General	Reading Main Line East	'Castle' (85A)	6 Worcester 7 Didcot (detached at Reading)	
16.45	Hereford	5	OOC	Oxford	—	'Castle' (85A)	6 Hereford 3 Stourbridge Jct	
16.48	High Wycombe	4	Yard	West Drayton	W Drayton East	61xx	5 non-corridor	
16.55	Cheltenham Spa	1	OOC	Kemble	—	'Castle' (85B)	9	'Cheltenham Spa Express'
17.00	Weston-super-Mare	2	OOC	Bath Spa	—	'Castle' (82A)	11	
17.06	Weston-super-Mare	5	OOC	Reading General	—	'Hall' (81A)	6 Weston-super-Mare 4 Didcot	advertised 17.05
17.10	Wolverhampton	3	OOC	Leamington Spa	Subway Junction	'King' (84A)	11 Wolverhampton 1 Bicester North (slip)	
17.15	Henley	4	WL	Maidenhead	Twyford East	'Hall'	8	
17.20	Reading General	1	WL	Slough	Slough West	'Hall' (81D)	2 corridors 5 non-corridors 1 corridor	
17.30	Plymouth	2	OOC	Taunton	—	'King' or 'Castle' (83D)	7 Plymouth 4 Kingswear	
17.35	Didcot	5	Yard	Langley	Reading Main Line East	'Hall'	9	
17.40	Windsor	1	WL	Iver	Slough Middle	61xx	5 non-corridor 1 corridor	
17.45	High Wycombe	6	Yard	West Drayton	Slough West	61xx	9 non-corridor	
17.50	Swansea	2	OOC	Newport	—	'Britannia' (86C)	5 Cardiff 2 Swansea 6 Carmarthen	Q
17.55	Carmarthen	3	OOC	Swindon	—			'The Red Dragon'
18.00	Weymouth	4	OOC	Newbury	—	'Castle' (81A)	7 Weymouth Town 4 Trowbridge (detached Newbury)	
18.05	Oxford	1	OOC	Reading General	—	'Castle' (81F)	6 Oxford 6 Didcot (detached Reading)	
18.08	Wolverhampton	6			Old Oak Common West			Q

18.10	Birkenhead	2	OOC	Bicester North	'King' (84A)	Old Oak Common West	6 Wolverhampton 6 Birkenhead	18.11 when 18.08 running
18.15	Henley	3	WL	Taplow	'Hall' (81D)	Slough West	10 (including 4 non-corridors)	
18.19	Bristol	5	WL Yard	Bath Spa	'Hall'		10	Q Fo *18.23 from Plat 4 when
18.20	Reading	5*		West Drayton		W Drayton East	5 non-corridor 3 corridor	18.19 running
18.30	Weston-super-Mare	1	OOC	Chippenham	'King' (81A)		Van +9	

Notes:

ECS Empty coaching stock
RL   Relief line
WL   West London Sidings
OOC Old Oak Common
Q   Ran when required
Fo   Fridays only

Shed codes:

81A Old Oak Common
81D Reading
81F Oxford
82A Bristol (Bath Road)
83D Plymouth (Laira)
84A Wolverhampton (Stafford Road)
85A Worcester
85B Gloucester
86C Cardiff (Canton)

Most of the night express freights to Penzance, Bristol, Cardiff, etc, started from Paddington Goods, on the up side just west of the passenger station. A pair of lines emanated from the depot, and the express goods would cross to the down main or down relief line at one of the several crossovers between Subway junction and Old Oak Common, and then usually pull into a loop at Old Oak Common or Acton to await its path on the down main.

A number of through long-distance freight trains started or terminated at Old Oak Common marshalling yard, while a spur from the North London line at Acton Wells junction brought many inter-Regional freights to Acton Yard. The Western Region had two more goods depots off its usual territory. Tank engines fitted with steam condensers worked trains between Acton and Smithfield depot, under the meat market, via the Metropolitan Line, and other trips were made from Old Oak Common to South Lambeth via Kensington Olympia.

Milk trains ran to the depots at West Ealing, Wood Lane (reached via Hanwell West loop and Park Royal), and to Kensington Olympia for disposal to various depots on the Southern Region. Parcels trains were mainly loaded at the parcels platform extending west of Platform 1 at Paddington, and unloaded in one of the station arrival platforms which are next to a roadway.

Acton to Twyford

There are four tracks for through trains the whole way from Paddington to Reading General (and beyond, but only on the Bristol line). Fast and slow lines are known on the Western Region as main and relief lines respectively, and their positions, from the south side, are down main, up main, down relief, up relief. In the 1950s there were one or more goods lines at various stages, mainly east of Slough.

Colour-light signals had been in operation between Paddington and Southall since the early 1930s, but worked on the block system and showing the same aspects as semaphore signals. Multiple-aspect signals were introduced between Acton and Hayes & Harlington in two stages in 1953 and 1955, but even so all existing signalboxes were retained except in the Ealing area where a panel at West Ealing replaced three other boxes on the main line. West of Hayes all the signals were semaphore until the 1960s.

Between Paddington and Reading six passenger branch lines left the main line in the 1950s, at West Ealing (for Greenford); two at West Drayton & Yiewsley (for Uxbridge and Staines West); at Slough (for Windsor & Eton Central); Maidenhead (for High Wycombe) and Twyford (for Henley). The Staines branch used the same tracks as the Uxbridge branch out of West Drayton to the north, then diverged and passed through a bridge under the main line. On most of the branches an ex-Great Western railcar or an auto train provided the basic service. From Henley two express trains, worked by 'Halls', ran to Paddington in the morning rush hour and returned in the evening.

Above: *'Castle' class No 5082* Swordfish, *piloted by an unidentified 'Hall', crosses the River Colne near West Drayton on 4 March 1961 with the 12.05 special from Paddington to Newbury Racecourse.* M. Pope

Below: *Shortly after Nationalisation Class U No 31804 descends the spur from Reading New junction to the Southern line with the through Birkenhead to Margate train via Guildford and Redhill, which it has probably taken over at Reading General from a WR engine. The train in the background is on the Paddington main line.* M. W. Earley

Above: *On 11 February 1956, a day of snow showers, Class U No 31799 of Guildford shed passes Reading General on the up through line with a freight train for the Southern Region.* R. C. Riley

Reading

There were three stations at Reading, called after Nationalisation, General, South, and West. Reading South, the Southern Region terminus adjacent to Reading General, was used by the electric trains from Waterloo and steam trains from the Redhill line. There were three connections between the Regions, two spurs joining the Western Region main line east of Reading General, and one underneath the main line to the Low Level goods depot. The only connection in regular use by passenger trains was the easternmost of the spurs, constructed during World War 2 and joining the Paddington line at Reading New Junction. This was traversed every weekday by the through Birkenhead to Margate train.

At the west end of Reading General is the junction between the Bristol and West of England main lines. In the 1950s, before it was resignalled for two-way working on all lines, Reading General had a main line platform and a relief platform line for each direction, numerous bay platforms, including three at the west end for local trains to and from Basingstoke and Newbury, and goods lines which bypassed the station to the north but did not connect with the West of England line. There was a through line between the down and up main platform lines which could be used by up trains only. A nonstop express for Paddington, whether from the West of England or the Bristol line, could without difficulty overtake another express which stopped at Reading. But down nonstop trains were often delayed by the lack of an overtaking line, all down expresses having to pass through Platform 4 (the down main). If a train at Platform 4 had to be overtaken, the following express could do it only by switching to the down relief line outside Reading, which involved crossing the up main line. For instance, in mid-

afternoon the down main platform was occupied every day for some 20 minutes by an express parcels train for Plymouth (via Bristol), and the following 14.35 Paddington to Weston-super-Mare, which stopped at Reading, had to cross from the down main to the down relief platform to get past.

The western approaches to Reading General were controlled by Reading Main Line West signalbox (still standing, and used as an office). The signal gantry included slip distant signals for each up platform, controlled by the East box, which told the guard of a train having to slip coaches at Reading whether conditions were favourable, in other words whether the road was clear through the station. If not, the train had to stop. An up train slipping at Reading (the only one from the West of England in the 1950s was the 08.30 Plymouth shortly before 13.00) passed through the platform line, so that the slip guard could bring the coach to a halt in the platform.

When a down West of England express slowed for the curve out of Reading General, and turned due south for the next couple of miles, it was passing along one side of a triangle formed also by the Bristol line and the spur connecting the two. In this triangle (on the site of the present diesel depot) was Reading locomotive shed. The spur, or west curve, joined the Berks & Hants line at Oxford Road junction, the signalbox being at the London end of Reading West station. Every weekday the through trains from Bournemouth to Birkenhead and York stopped at the wooden platforms of this station, their next stops being Oxford to the north or Basingstoke to the south. In the summer the York train was extended to and from Newcastle. Southern Region engines — 'West Country' and 'Battle of Britain' Pacifics and 'King Arthurs' for the most part, or sometimes a 'Lord Nelson' — hauled these trains as far as Oxford. The prewar daily service between Wolverhampton and Portsmouth had dwindled to summer Fridays and Saturdays only in the 1950s.

Other Southern engines passed regularly through

Reading West on transfer freight trains from Moreton Cutting yard, near Didcot, to Basingstoke. Many other freights joined the Berks & Hants at Oxford Road junction, including most of those originating at Reading for the West of England main line, which were marshalled in the yards at Reading West junction on the Bristol line, and a number running between the Midlands, especially the Birmingham area, and Basingstoke. A regular perishables train from Worcester to Eastleigh was scheduled to pass through Reading West shortly before 22.00.

All trains for Basingstoke and the Southern Region branch off at Southcote junction, a mile further on. These included not only the inter-Regional freights and expresses already mentioned, but stopping trains between Reading General and Basingstoke every one or two hours, some of which ran to and from Portsmouth & Southsea or Southampton Terminus. In the evening stopping trains arrived from Bournemouth West and from Weymouth, the latter terminating after midnight.

Just before Southcote junction a single track leaves the main line on the down side, and leads back to Reading Central goods depot at Coley, almost in the middle of the town. Twice a day in the 1950s an engine made a trip from the yards at Reading West Junction to Central Goods, shunting at each end in between.

Newbury

The race course at Newbury is on the London side of the town and has its own station with four platforms and a signalbox. There are two additional platforms besides those on the main line, and independent sidings connect the Race Course station with Newbury Town. In steam days the only turntable in Newbury was at Race Course station.

Race meetings are held about once a month throughout the year, both flat racing and steeplechasing. On race days in the 1950s the station became busy before 09.00 as local trains, at first in the down direction, made special stops. Two extra signalboxes were opened for the day between Reading and Newbury, one of them at Bulls Lock, between Thatcham and Newbury Race Course. Even some expresses stopped specially at Race Course; two were Weymouth trains, the 12.30 Paddington and the 09.00 Weymouth; while racegoers from the west were set down by the 08.30 Plymouth to Paddington, and could return by the 15.30 Paddington to Penzance.

Up to five special trains ran from Paddington to Newbury Race Course, the majority coming down nonstop in an hour or just over. The most important was the Members' and First Class special, a 13-coach train regularly hauled by a 'King' and conveying two separate dining cars at different ends of the train, one for members only and the other for ordinary first class passengers. The doors were kept locked between the members' coaches and the rest of the train. Wherever this train was mentioned in the special working notice for the Races it appeared in bold type. In the 1950s the Members' special usually included some vintage coaching stock, such as Great Western 70-foot brake firsts of 1910 built for Fishguard boat trains.

'Castle' class engines were usually provided for the

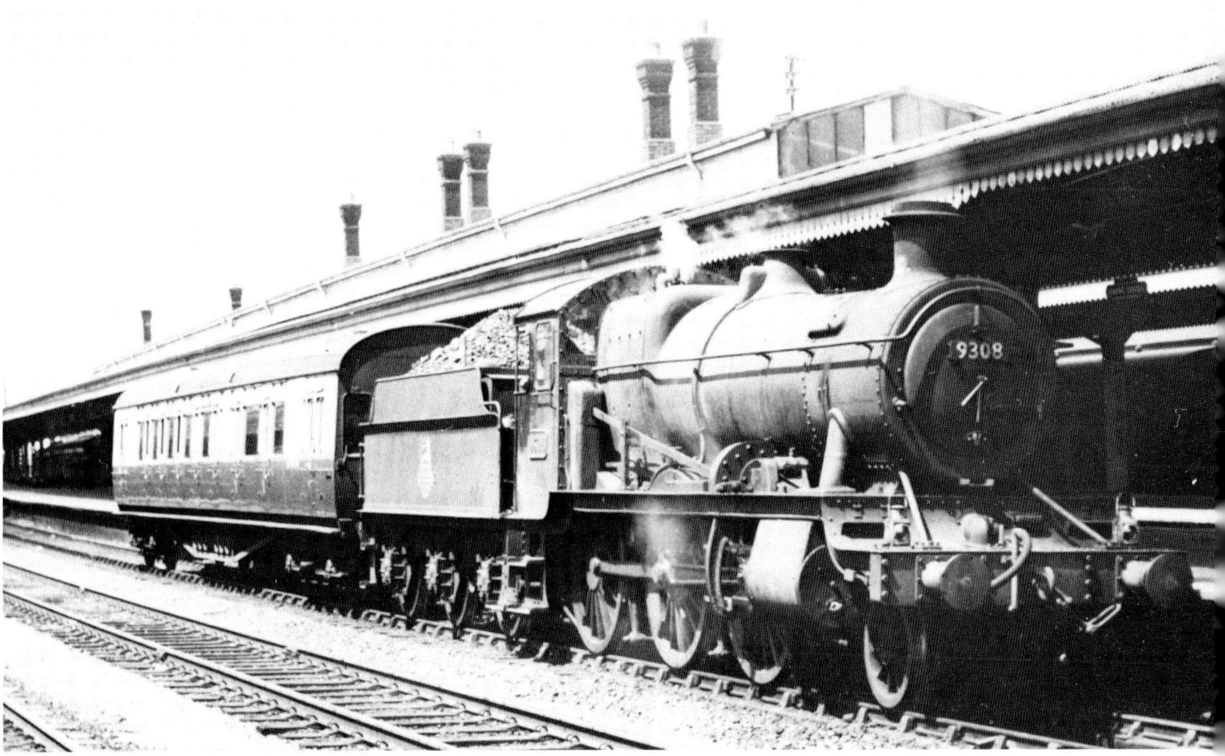

Above left: *In the summer of 1949 the 08.30 Plymouth to Paddington (later to be named the 'Mayflower') slipped a coach at Reading General on each weekday, although subsequently it was retimed to call at Reading on summer Saturdays. On Saturday 25 June 1949, No 6023* King Edward II *has run through Platform 5 and is rejoining the up main line at Reading Main Line East box. Going out of the picture to the left is the older of the two spurs to the Southern Region.* C. C. B. Herbert

Above: *The Reading General station pilot, Class 43xx No 9308, carrying express passenger headlamps, removes from Platform 5 a coach which has been slipped by an up express. Photographed on Monday 4 July 1955.* R. L. Evans

Right: *The junction between the Bristol and Berks & Hants routes at Reading. Although bound for Plymouth, this 1950 express hauled by No 6022* King Edward III *pulls out of Platform 4 and takes the Bristol line at Reading Main Line West box.* M. W. Earley

other Paddington specials, and a standby engine was kept at Paddington all morning, and one at Newbury Race Course in the afternoon, in case of engine failure on any of the race trains.

Special trains ran to Newbury Races from other parts. For the August meeting in 1957, for example, held on Friday 16th and Saturday 17th, a special ran from Acton on both days, calling at the principal stations east of Reading. Only suburban non-corridor stock could be spared for this train on the Saturday. On both days a special arrived at Newbury via the Compton line from Oxford or Banbury; at Newbury Town this train had to reverse and was worked to and from Race Course by the Newbury pilot engine. There was a buffet car special from Cardiff which ran either by way of Devizes or via the east chord at Westbury. Each day after the last race a 3-coach special ran from Newbury Race Course to Taunton, calling at a number of stations such as Somerton, from where racegoers could get to the course by changing from the Castle Cary auto train into the 09.00 Weymouth to Paddington, but could not get home by a regular service.

Race Course station by no means returned to complete stillness between meetings. At night many of the down freights stopped there for examination of the train, making use of the sidings so as to leave the main line clear. The sidings were also used for the shunting of wagons between some of the night freight trains, and an engine was on duty at Race Course all night for this purpose. Bull's Lock signalbox, already mentioned, was normally open only at night. In an emergency Race Course station was a convenient place to change engines if a train suffered a failure in the area, and for turning an engine. In fact, there being no turntable at Newbury Town, Race Course had some regular turning duties. One was the 'Hall' from Reading shed which ran light to Hungerford in the early morning to work the 07.20 to Paddington, and was turned at Newbury Race Course on the way down; another, around midday, was a Southern engine in between working a passenger train from Eastleigh to Newbury (via Whitchurch) and back.

Newbury Town station has a through line and a platform line in each direction, plus bay platforms for local trains on the up side facing east and on the down side facing west. The Lambourn branch bay faced west on the up side. There were three signalboxes, Newbury East junction, Middle and West. At East junction the Didcot, Newbury & Southampton line came in from the direction of Compton, and left the main line towards Whitchurch Town and Winchester Chesil at Enborne junction, one mile west of Newbury. Most of the passenger trains on this line were through trains between Didcot and Southampton Terminus (but stopped short at Eastleigh with the coming of the 'Hampshire' diesels in 1957); one train in the afternoon started from Oxford. Many of them in each direction had long waits at Newbury; the usual procedure was to stop at the main platform and, having set down passengers for Newbury, pull forward and reverse into the bay in order to await a connection with a main line stopping train or a Weymouth express. One or two of the main line stopping

trains also moved into the bay platform at Newbury to make way for a faster train. In the morning for instance, the 07.10 Westbury to Reading was overtaken by and connected with the 07.15 Trowbridge to Paddington; later, in the other direction, the 12.43 Reading to Westbury was shunted for half-an-hour and connected with the 12.30 Paddington to Weymouth.

The line between Didcot and Newbury was doubled during World War 2, when it became a trunk route for D-Day traffic to the south coast, and remained double thereafter. From Enborne junction the section to Winchester, which became part of the Southern Region in 1950, was double-track only as far as Woodhay, the first station. Passenger trains were usually three coaches hauled in the early 1950s mostly by Class 2251 0-6-0s from Didcot shed, but from 1953 onwards the workings were shared with Southern Region engines from Eastleigh, mainly Class T9 4-4-0s or Standard Class 4 2-6-0s. There were pick-up goods trains, and through freights to and from Banbury and Wolverhampton, which either stayed on the main line and made for Westbury or the West of England, or turned off at Enborne junction and went to Eastleigh. In the late 1950s and early 1960s there were regular fitted freights from Southampton Docks to the Midlands and heavy oil trains from Fawley refinery. The line remained open for the oil traffic until 1964, two years after the last section had been closed to passengers, and the trains from Fawley were often hauled by Standard Class 9F 2-10-0 engines.

The Lambourn branch train had its own bay platform at Newbury and its own single track adjacent to the main line for half a mile before turning away to the north. The branch had been opened under a Light Railway Order, and since 1937 had been worked mainly by a Great Western diesel railcar, one of the later type capable of hauling tail traffic. The Lambourn line served a number of racing stables, and the railcar was allowed to pull up to six horseboxes; on some journeys it worked with a trailer coach. The railcar was kept at Reading, and in the 1950s worked to Thatcham in the early morning as an unadvertised passenger train, then on to Hungerford carrying newspapers and parcels only; it returned empty to Newbury to begin its duties on the Lambourn branch. The last passenger train of the day terminated at Lambourn, after which the railcar ran empty all the way to Reading, but it could be ordered to carry passengers from Newbury and call at all stations to Reading if the 19.20 Trowbridge to Reading stopping train was running late. There was a daily goods train from Newbury to

Above: *The 11.48 Westbury to Reading
General (via Devizes) stopping train calls
at Newbury on 5 March 1960 behind
No 4962* Ragley Hall. R. C. Riley

Right: *The single track of the Lambourn
branch ran parallel with the main line on
the up side for half-a-mile west of
Newbury. On 28 September 1957
Class 57xx No 4665 emerges from the bay
and passes Newbury West box with the
14.00 to Lambourn.* Ian Allan Library

Above: *The 15.30 Paddington to Penzance and Kingswear, hauled by No 6012* King Edward VI, *passes Brewham signalbox, the summit of the line between Westbury and Taunton, on 9 July 1956. The train is now without its Weymouth portion, which will have been slipped at Heywood Road junction near Westbury, and this portion will pass Brewham in about 20 minutes time attached to the 16.25 from Bristol.* R. C. Riley

Left: *In August 1950 what looks like a Class 43xx 2-6-0 passes Wolfhall junction on the 11.22 stopping train from Bristol to Reading via Devizes. The former Midland & South Western Junction line to Andover can be seen on the extreme left, and the picture appears to have been taken from the rail overbridge leading to Savernake (High Level) station.* B. Canning

Lambourn and back, whose engine then hauled an afternoon passenger train to Lambourn and returned light or with the empty coaches. This was the only passenger working of the day not rostered for the diesel railcar; the engine was from Reading shed, and in the early 1950s would probably be one of the last surviving ex-Midland & South Western 2-4-0s or Dean Goods 0-6-0s. Subsequently the Class 2251 and the '57xx' pannier tanks were permitted. For most of the 1950s the branch was closed on Sundays.

Savernake (Low Level)

Savernake must be one of the few British railway stations to have been named after a forest. Where now there is no station, in the 1950s there were two, and the network of lines, of which only cuttings and embankments remain, needs some historical introduction. In 1864 the Great Western Railway built a single line branch from Savernake through the forest to Marlborough. Twenty years later the Midland & South Western Junction

Railway was formed to make a through route from Cheltenham to Southampton, parts of which were already in existence. The through route was completed in 1891; it had its own station at Marlborough, then joined the Great Western branch and used the Great Western station at Savernake, leaving the main line at Wolf Hall to continue towards Ludgershall and Andover. The once complicated layout around Savernake was the result of the obstructive tactics of the Great Western in delaying Midland & South Western trains between Marlborough and Savernake. A company was promoted to build a railway from Marlborough to Savernake independent of the Great Western system. On this line, opened in 1898, a separate Savernake station was built, later to be known as High Level, and the new line crossed the Great Western on a bridge and rejoined the Midland & South-Western near East Grafton. Finally the Great Western in 1905 built a spur from their main line to allow through running between Paddington and Tidworth (on a branch from Ludgershall).

At the 1923 Grouping the Great Western took control of this part of the Midland & South Western, and 10 years later made some economies on the duplicate lines from Marlborough to Savernake. The line of the Great Western branch to Marlborough and its terminus station were abandoned, the branch trains using instead the former northbound track of the Midland & South Western as a single line, and terminating at the MSWJ station. The MSWJ line was singled, using the former southbound track, and at Savernake (High Level) all trains were to use the former northbound platform, the other to be a loop for goods trains only.

The layout remained the same from 1933 almost to the end of the 1950s. From the east, the first junction was reached just after the main line curves past Crofton pumping station. This was Grafton East junction, where up and down tracks diverged to the left to join the Midland & South Western in the direction of Ludgershall. The connection, known as Grafton curve, had no regular traffic in the 1950s and the signalbox was normally switched out; in 1957 the curve was closed altogether. Next the main line passed under a bridge carrying the single track of the direct MSWJ line from Savernake (High Level) to Grafton South Junction (south of which the line was double-track as far as its junction with the Southern near Andover). At Wolfhall junction the original MSWJ line from Grafton South junction to Savernake (Low Level) joined the main line, the connection being double-track except on a bridge over the Kennet & Avon Canal. Savernake (Low Level) had up and down platforms and a bay on the up side facing west for the ex-Great Western Marlborough branch trains. There were two signalboxes at the station, the Marlborough branch diverging to the right at Savernake West box.

Until 1958 there were two through trains a day in each direction between Cheltenham and Southampton Terminus, and other trains between Cheltenham or Swindon and Andover Junction. Two of the five southbound trains and one of the four northbound ran via Savernake (Low Level), some Midland & South Western

trains having been re-routed this way in 1933. In the summer of 1958 the service was reduced and shortly afterwards all remaining passenger trains were diverted via Low Level.

Freight trains ran between Cheltenham or Swindon and the Southern Region, mostly hauled by Class 43xx 2-6-0s. All the Midland & South Western line freights used the High Level route at Savernake, the only exception being the pick-up goods between Westbury and Ludgershall, which used the connection from Wolfhall Junction to Grafton South Junction.

The Marlborough branch train ran up and down seven or eight times a day, starting from the bay platform at Savernake (Low Level). It usually consisted of a Class 45xx tank engine pulling a 'B' set, the standard pair of permanently coupled non-corridor coaches used on Western Region branch lines. Connections from the Reading and Newbury direction were good. Of the Weymouth expresses, the 18.00 Paddington (main portion) and the 16.10 Weymouth called at Savernake (Low Level), as also the two morning trains to Paddington from Trowbridge and Frome and the 14.35 Paddington to Weston-super-Mare. On a Sunday evening there was a train to Paddington just before 19.00 which called at Reading only. This was originally a Penzance train but later started from Taunton; connecting with it was a stopping train from Trowbridge via Devizes which was shunted at Savernake (Low Level) and eventually also terminated at Paddington.

Patney & Chirton

The full name of this station was Patney & Chirton Junction. Here the new main line via Westbury left the original single track of the Berks & Hants Extension Railway to Devizes. The junction was at Patney & Chirton but the two lines remained close together for more than a mile. The up platform at Patney was an island; trains from Devizes ran to the outer face, which was connected to the up main line at both ends. The platform was used by the auto trains running to and from Devizes and Westbury, and could also be used if a stopping train arrived from the Devizes line and had to wait for a late running express before it could proceed. In the mornings an auto train arrived from Trowbridge via Devizes and connected into the 08.15 Frome to Paddington which had come via Lavington; went to Devizes and back, connecting in the up direction into the 09.27 Westbury to Reading stopper via Lavington; and finally departed for Lavington and Westbury shortly before 10.00, connecting with the morning Reading-Devizes-Bristol stopping train. Another auto made a journey to Warminster and back and left Patney for good at about midday, at one time running through to Bath. Auto trains did not visit Patney for the rest of the day except in the early 1950s when one made an afternoon journey from Trowbridge and returned to Westbury.

Westbury

The Westbury avoiding line diverges from the earlier main line through Westbury station at Heywood Road

junction, although of the two the avoiding line passes nearer the town. As at Reading, Heywood Road down distant gantry had a slip distant signal. There were three signalboxes at Westbury station, called North, Middle and South (following the general alignment of the Wilts, Somerset & Weymouth Railway). At Westbury North the main line was joined by the lines from Bristol and Swindon, which had already met north of Trowbridge. Westbury station has two island platforms, numbered from the south 1 and 2 for down trains and 3 and 4 for up trains, and a goods line for each direction avoiding the station. Platforms 1 and 3 are normally used by Salisbury line trains, which leave the West of England and

Weymouth lines at Westbury South and climb to a summit at Upton Scudamore, passing over the avoiding line. The Westbury station line and the avoiding line meet again at Fairwood junction. A double-track connection, known as the east chord, enables a train to run without reversal from the London direction at Heywood Road junction to Trowbridge and eventually Bath and Bristol; the east chord joins the Westbury to Trowbridge line at Hawkeridge signalbox.

All the regular Weymouth trains stopped at Westbury, excluding some of the Channel Islands boat expresses. Only one down West of England express stopped, and two slipped coaches at Heywood Road; in the up direction three West of England expresses served Westbury, the first two in the morning running nonstop to Paddington.

A number of through trains ran daily between Portsmouth and Bristol or Cardiff, the chief of which was the Brighton to Cardiff train. On these cross-country trains 'Hall', 'Castle' and 'County' 4-6-0s from Bristol (Bath Road) or Cardiff (Canton) sheds worked to Salisbury and back (never beyond), and Canton sometimes used a 'Britannia' Pacific or a Standard Class 4MT 4-6-0. Freight trains on the route, mainly from the Bristol area or carrying coal from South Wales, were handled by Class 28xx or 'WD' 2-8-0s, together with the '43xx' 2-6-0s. Stopping trains ran between Salisbury or Westbury and Bristol or Swindon; auto trains puffed to and fro between Westbury and Chippenham, Trowbridge, Patney & Chirton, Devizes, Warminster and Frome. During the night a number of main line freights ran via Westbury instead of the avoiding line, and stopped for water, examination of the train or a change of crew. Two up trains which stopped at Westbury and then took the Trowbridge line were the 18.35 Weymouth to Kensington milk and the 23.20 Taunton to Wolverhampton express parcels; for most of the 1950s the Weymouth milk travelled up to London by the original route via Chippenham.

The east chord between Heywood Road junction and

Top left: Pannier tank No 3739 hauls two corridors on a Chippenham to Westbury local on 8 June 1964, taking the place of a diesel railcar which has failed. The train is crossing the junction (controlled by Westbury North box) with the lines from Heywood Road. The embankment carrying Westbury east chord can just be picked out in the distance. Derek Cross

Centre left: On 15 June 1963 'Castle' No 5043 Earl of Mount Edgcumbe *leaves Platform 3 at Westbury and passes North box with the 16.33 Salisbury to Bristol; and 'Hall' No 6930* Aldersey Hall *stands in Platform 4 with the 17.25 Westbury to Swindon. The up goods line is to the right of the Swindon train, and both trains are carrying Class B (stopping passenger) headlamps.* Gerald T. Robinson

Bottom left: A typical summer Saturday extra. With reporting number chalked on twice and a number of Eastern Region carriages, Class 43xx No 6352 of Cardiff (Canton) shed hauling the 09.00 Cardiff to Portsmouth & Southsea on 16 July 1955 is banked out of Westbury on the climb to Upton Scudamore by Class 56xx tank No 5689. The Class 43xx will come off the train at Salisbury. R. E. Toop

Below: Fairwood junction on August Bank Holiday Saturday 1952. A down stopping train for Weymouth, believed to be the 12.45 from Bristol, approaches the junction with the Westbury avoiding line behind Class 43xx 2-6-0 No 7300. G. J. Jefferson

Above: Class 47xx No 4705 of Southall shed performs some shunting at Westbury with the 14.00 Acton Yard to Hackney Class D freight on 15 June 1963. The engine is on the exit from the down goods line to the Salisbury line at South box, and before departing will have to set back behind the signalbox and cross to the West of England line which goes out of picture to the left. Gerald T. Robinson

Hawkeridge was not in regular use by passenger trains although it was not infrequently employed as a diversionary route. But for most of the 1950s it was used by certain night freights between the London area and Bristol, such as the 20.05 express freight from Paddington, and by two milk trains. In the down direction the milk empties from Wood Lane to Whitland passed this way en route for the Severn Tunnel; likewise the Wellington to West Ealing milk train, running via Bristol, Bath and Trowbridge.

Frome

The Frome avoiding line begins at Clink Road junction, a little over three miles from the end of the Westbury avoiding line, and the distance between has always been one block section. Unlike at Westbury, where the avoiding line is fractionally longer than the line through the station, the Frome avoiding line saves nearly a quarter of a mile. The Frome station line, which was double track throughout the 1950s, rejoins the avoiding line at Blatchbridge junction. On the London side of Frome station a branch line, the North Somerset, ran north-west towards Radstock West and Bristol. The branch, which was nearly all single track, had a passenger traffic until 1959, and served a number of stone quarries on the edge of the Mendip Hills and collieries in the Radstock area. It could be approached both from the station and, by freight trains only, from the east by a connection known as the mineral loop. So a down train via Frome first reached Frome North signalbox, at the start of the mineral loop, then Frome South, where the branch passenger trains turned off. The two spurs combined into a single track, the third junction being controlled by a ground frame. The mineral loop was sometimes used by main line freight trains for attaching or detaching wagons or allowing an express to pass on the avoiding line.

Frome station had up and down main platforms and a bay on the up side for the branch trains. Nearly all the

Weymouth trains stopped there, but not normally the West of England expresses. The following is a list of the main line passenger trains which called in the summer of 1955 (Mondays to Fridays):

Up Trains

Arrive	Depart	Description
	06.30	Westbury Auto
	07.06	Chippenham auto
	08.15	Paddington semi-fast
08.53	08.56	08.35 Bruton-Westbury
09.30	09.32	07.17 Weymouth-Chippenham slow
09.43	09.44	08.15 Weymouth-Bristol semi-fast
10.36	10.40	09.00 Weymouth-Paddington
12.09	12.12	10.33 Weymouth-Wolverhampton
13.34	13.39	11.40 Weymouth-Swindon slow
14.12	14.14	12.35 Weymouth-Bristol semi-fast
15.19	15.22	13.40 Weymouth-Westbury semi-fast
16.42	16.45	14.33 Weymouth-Westbury slow
17.27	17.33	15.40 Weymouth Quay-Paddington
17.42	17.48	16.10 Weymouth-Paddington
18.31	—	17.00 Taunton auto
18.46	18.48	16.37 Taunton-Trowbridge via Yeovil
20.20	20.26	19.00 Taunton-Westbury auto
20.36	20.41	18.10 Weymouth-Westbury slow
21.11	21.14	19.30 Weymouth-Bristol semi-fast

Down Trains

Arrive	Depart	Description
06.54	06.56	06.45 Westbury-Taunton auto
07.24	07.29	05.45 Bristol-Weymouth slow
08.03	08.05	07.45 Trowbridge-Bruton
09.12	09.14	08.05 Bristol-Weymouth semi-fast
09.36	09.38	09.27 Westbury-Weymouth slow
10.41	10.43	08.30 Weston-super-Mare-Weymouth semi-fast
12.56	13.00	11.45 Chippenham-Weymouth slow*
14.55	15.03	12.30 Paddington-Weymouth
15.38	15.41	11.15 Wolverhampton-Weymouth
16.25	16.27	16.15 Westbury-Weymouth slow
17.33	17.35	16.25 Bristol-Weymouth semi-fast*
17.54	17.57	17.10 Melksham-Taunton auto
18.17	18.19	17.02 Bristol-Weymouth slow
20.39	20.42	18.00 Paddington-Weymouth
21.00	21.04	20.50 Westbury-Weymouth passenger and milk empties
22.25	—	22.15 Westbury auto

* included slip coach from Paddington

The best trains between Frome and Bristol via Trowbridge and Bath took just over an hour. The North Somerset branch struck a more direct course for Bristol, and was nearly 10 miles shorter; most of its stopping trains, of which there were eight a day in each direction in the 1950s, also took just over an hour. But the North Somerset had one regular express, and this is the explanation why the Channel Islands Boat Express called at Frome in the up direction instead of Westbury. Passengers from Bristol to Guernsey and Jersey caught the 08.30 Weston-super-Mare to Weymouth at 09.26 and connected into the boat train at Westbury; coming back, however, they changed at Frome into the 17.55 for Bristol via the North Somerset branch, which carried express headlamps and stopped at Radstock West and Pensford only.

The North Somerset branch train normally consisted of a 'B' set hauled by a '45xx' 2-6-2T or a '57xx' pannier tank, although the 17.55 Frome could load to seven coaches in the summer. Diesel railcars made occasional journeys, and in 1958 Standard Class 3 2-6-2T engines began to take a share in the workings. Some of the branch trains made a circuit, continuing down the main line to Witham, and returning to Bristol via Wells and Yatton. The engine workings were shared by Bristol (Bath Road) and Frome Sheds. Frome was a subshed to Westbury and had an allocation of eight tank engines, which covered the branch trains, the two Frome station pilots, and pannier tank trips to one of the stone quarries. On bank holidays excursion trains ran to Weston-super-Mare or the Glamorgan coast, starting at Frome and usually picking up at the intermediate stations. Sometimes the excursion was the 10.50 Frome regular train extended beyond Bristol. These trains usually consisted of a Class 43xx 2-6-0 and six to eight coaches.

Witham

The next station after Frome was Witham, where a single line branch diverged on the up side via Wells and Cheddar to Yatton, on the main line between Taunton and Bristol. This was really two branch lines, opened at

Below: *Class 57xx No 3773 stands in the bay at Witham with a train for Yatton via the East Somerset branch, formed of a B set. The up main platform is occupied by what appears to be another B set on a train to Frome, probably having come from Yatton by the same route.* R. E. Toop

different stages, the East Somerset from Witham to Wells and the Cheddar Valley from Wells to Yatton. Those branch trains which terminated at Witham used a roofed bay platform on the up side, the station otherwise having the usual down and up main line platforms. The engines and trains were not dissimilar to those on the North Somerset branch; indeed, as has been mentioned, some made a round trip from Bristol using both branches.

In the 1950s there were four or five passenger trains a day in each direction between Witham and Wells, of which nearly all ran through to Yatton and about half were through Bristol trains. At the Witham end over half the trains started or terminated at Frome. Local goods trains ran to and from Wells and Cheddar, and this branch, like the North Somerset, served a number of quarries of Mendip stone. In addition there was traffic in strawberries, mainly from Axbridge, Cheddar and Draycott; often in the season vans were attached to passenger trains, but at one period there was a timetable path for a complete trainload to run when required to Birmingham (Moor Street), leaving Axbridge in the late evening and travelling via Witham, Trowbridge and Swindon.

The passenger trains on the branch in the 1950s consisted again mainly of 'B' sets, worked by '45xx' or '57xx' tank engines. During the mid-1950s Ivatt Class 2 2-6-0s of the London Midland Region, based at one of the Bristol sheds, worked most of the freights and some passenger trains. There was a turn for a diesel railcar, which left Bristol after lunch, made a trip from Yatton to Clevedon and back, then to Frome via Wells and Witham, returning to Bristol by the North Somerset line.

Right: On 16 May 1964 Class 45xx No 4591 calls at Lyng Halt, on the single-track between Athelney and Durston, with the 12.37 Yeovil (Pen Mill) to Taunton. A month later the Yeovil branch was closed to passengers and the line through Lyng Halt closed completely. M. J. Fox

Centre right: The same coaches return from Taunton on the 14.10 to Yeovil, seen at Langport West behind No 4593. The branch was double-track to this point from its junction with the main line at Curry Rivel, and the fireman has no doubt just collected the single line token. W. G. Sumner

Brewham-Taunton

Just after Bruton a westbound express, racing down from Brewham summit, passed under a bridge carrying the Somerset & Dorset line, near its own station at Cole. Then at Castle Cary the Weymouth line, formerly double track throughout, turned away to the south. Castle Cary has an up and down platform and up and down goods loops to the east of the station. Here some of the through freight trains stopped for traffic or to allow a passenger express to overtake, while for most of the day an engine, usually from Yeovil shed, was on duty to bank eastbound goods trains, when required, up the longish climb to Brewham. The down Plymouth milk empties stopped at Castle Cary to uncouple tanks for the Weymouth line (later attached to the 20.50 Westbury), and while it was in the down loop the 17.30 Paddington to Plymouth was scheduled to pass through. Most of the Weymouth trains, stopping or express, called at Castle Cary, but to reach the West of England you had to set out on the Taunton push-and-pull (or make for the Southern Region at Yeovil

Left: *A 'Castle' heads through Somerton and across the viaduct over the River Cary with an up West of England express on the afternoon of Saturday 2 July 1955.*
R. C. Riley

Right: *On 17 August 1961 Class 45xx No 5571 leaves Lyng Halt and is about to pass under the Taunton road with a Yeovil (Pen Mill) to Taunton train.*
Michael J. Fox

Junction). For the most part the Taunton trains terminated at Castle Cary; of the remainder, some were shunted to connect with Weymouth trains. For instance, the first down train of the day, starting from Westbury, was shunted at Castle Cary for 50 minutes to connect with the 05.45 Bristol to Weymouth: the evening train from Melksham to Taunton was shunted for half-an-hour to connect with the 17.02 from Bristol.

The small town of Langport in Somerset had two stations. The first, which became Langport West, was on the Bristol & Exeter Railway branch from Taunton to Yeovil. When the new West of England main line was laid from Castle Cary, it joined the Yeovil branch at Curry Rivel junction, just west of Langport, and a new East station was built on the main line. The Yeovil branch was single-track except between Langport West and Curry Rivel junction.

In the 1950s the train service from Langport to Taunton was slightly better at the branch line station, with seven passenger trains in each direction, and an extra journey in the summer on Saturday evenings. There was no Sunday service from either station. Nearly all the trains started or terminated at Yeovil (Pen Mill), but a late afternoon train from Taunton ran through to Trowbridge (via Yeovil and Castle Cary). The passenger trains usually consisted of a 'B' set, often strengthened with one or two corridor coaches, and hauled by a Class 45xx tank engine from Taunton or Yeovil shed. As on the Castle Cary trains, some engines worked through to and from Minehead.

Four miles west of Curry Rivel junction was Athelney station, surrounded by marsh land, where the final section of new main line was built at the beginning of this century to take a short cut to Taunton by way of Cogload. Here the single line of the old Yeovil branch turned off on the up side through Lyng Halt to join the Bristol & Exeter main line at Durston. The new cut-off was only a quarter of a mile shorter. For most of the 1950s three out of the five Castle Cary trains, and all but one of the more numerous Yeovil stoppers, went via Durston in each direction.

In 1932 a flyover was completed at Cogload, and the line quadrupled from there through Taunton to Norton Fitzwarren, where the Minehead and Barnstaple lines diverged from the main line. Cogload flyover carries the down Bristol line over the down and up Paddington lines. Continuing west the two middle lines (down and up Paddington) become the main or fast lines: the outer lines (down and up Bristol) become the relief or slow lines. At Cogload in the 1950s there was a crossover from the down Bristol line to the down main and from up main to up Bristol, but the first complete set of crossovers was at Creech junction, with another on each side of Taunton

Below: The 10.20 Kingswear to Liverpool and Manchester, with No 4932 Hatherton Hall, *passes Creech St Michael Halt on the up main on Saturday 13 September 1952.* R. H. G. Simpson

Right: On 15 July 1957 the 15.30 Paddington to Penzance, hauled by 'Castle' No 5071 Spitfire, *makes its first stop at Taunton, which will be in the down main platform. The train approaching on the down relief line may be the 17.04 from Chard Junction, which was due at about the same time, and if so will run to No 2 bay to the right of the camera.* R. E. Vincent

Below right: Class 45xx No 5504 departs from Taunton's Platform 7, the up relief line, with the 14.05 to Yeovil (Pen Mill), consisting of a B set strengthened with an extra coach. J. Davenport

153
PASSENGERS MU
NOT CROSS THE L
EXCEPT BY MEA
OF THE SUBWA

5504

station. Creech junction, where the Chard branch joined the main line, was west of Creech St Michael Halt; the halt had platforms on the relief lines only, inaccessible to trains taking the Paddington line at Cogload, and therefore a Yeovil or Castle Cary train using the cut-off had to run nonstop between Athelney and Taunton.

The Chard branch, whose trains are described in Part One, was single-track and joined the main line on the down side facing Taunton. There was no recognised crossing point between Creech junction and Chard Central, although in an emergency two trains were allowed to cross at Ilminster. At Taunton the Chard trains used No 2 bay at the London end on the down side. A down train could reach the bay easily from the down relief line, but up Chard trains had to cross both down lines to the up main, and very soon recross both down lines to gain their branch at Creech junction.

Taunton had four through platforms, two for each direction, and bay platforms for local trains at all four corners of the station. There were three signalboxes dealing with main line trains, East junction, West station and West junction. Most freight trains, up or down, used the pair of goods lines leaving the main lines at East junction, running behind the station on the down side past the engine shed, and rejoining the main lines one mile west of the station.

Taunton to Exeter

West of Cogload the railway is much busier, the London trains being joined by those from the Midlands, South Wales and the North of England, and a few more from London, all having travelled via Bristol. At summer weekends the line became very congested, and many works were carried out in the 1930s to increase its capacity. Apart from those in the Taunton area already

Above: Class 2251 0-6-0 No 3215 sets out from the down main platform (No 5) at Taunton on 15 July 1957 with the 15.30 to Minehead. The train will probably run relief line from West Station box to Norton Fitzwarren, junction for the branch. R. E. Vincent

Above right: Tiverton Junction was one of the stations between Taunton and Exeter to be rebuilt in the 1930s with four tracks for overtaking purposes. 'Castle' class No 7000 Viscount Portal *arrives at the down platform on the 18.20 Taunton to Exeter stopping train. The signal is off for the connecting train to Hemyock to depart from the branch platform on the extreme right and the Hemyock branch can be seen curving away behind the second coach.* J. Davenport

Right: The up 'Torbay Express' passes Wellington station on the through line behind 'Castle' No 5074 Hampden *on Saturday 6 July 1957, and the signal has already been replaced in the 'on' position.* R. C. Riley

mentioned, two wayside signalboxes were opened between Taunton and Exeter in order to shorten the block sections, and four of the intermediate stations, Sampford Peverell, Tiverton Junction, Cullompton and Stoke Canon, were rebuilt with separate through and platform lines so that stopping trains could be overtaken by holiday expresses.

For the stiff climb to Whiteball tunnel in the down direction, at least one banking engine was normally on duty at Wellington station, usually a Class 51xx tank; in winter most of the banker's work was with freight trains but on a summer weekend many heavy passenger trains would need assistance. Beyond Whiteball tunnel were sidings on both sides, in one of which the bank engine would wait until the up line was clear for its return to Wellington.

Below: *Six minutes later the 10.35 Paddington to Penzance and Falmouth approaches Wellington from the other direction with No 6027* King Richard I *and is signalled on the down through line. There are two bank engines on duty, Class 51xx Nos 4117 and 4139, but a 'King' did not usually stop for assistance even with 14 coaches.* R. C. Riley

Bottom: *On 4 September 1954 'Grange' class No 6848* Toddington Grange *passes Whiteball Siding box at the head of the 08.06 Sheffield to Kingswear. The signalbox was burned down the following year and replaced by the one shown in the following photograph. In the up siding is one of the bank engines, No 4136, evidently about to return to Wellington as the ground signal (partially visible behind the tank engine's bunker) and the up starter signal are 'off'.* R. C. Riley

Right: *No 6872* Crawley Grange *passes the new Whiteball Siding box and the bank engine siding on Saturday 21 July 1956 with the 16.15 Paignton to Paddington, which ran nonstop between Torquay and Slough. The 'Grange' was somewhat off its usual beat, being allocated to Pontypool Road shed.* R. C. Riley

Centre right: *With distants cleared, 'Modified Hall' No 6973* Bricklehampton Hall *passes Stoke Canon on the up through line on Saturday 6 July 1957 with the 10.10 Paignton to Cardiff.* R. C. Riley

Bottom right: *Both the Minehead and Barnstaple branches left the main line on the up side just west of Norton Fitzwarren. Class 51xx No 4136 approaches the station on the down main on 15 July 1955 with a train described by the photographer as a Barnstaple train, but almost certainly heading for Minehead, or even Exeter, as the '51xx' class was not permitted on the Barnstaple line.* S. Creer

Below: *On 26 August 1958 Class 45xx No 5563 enters Bishops Lydeard on the 10.50 Minehead to Taunton. The branch was double track from here to Norton Fitzwarren where it joined the main line.* Michael Hale

Bottom: *Class 2251 No 2212 leaves Crowcombe with an evening down stopping train to Minehead on Saturday 1 September 1951. The coaches appear to have roofboards and may have formed a through train from Paddington earlier in the day. The letter M on the buffer beam denoted Minehead and was a target carried at busy times mainly to help signalmen in the Taunton to Norton Fitzwarren area.* A. F. Taylor

Right: *Class 45xx No 5571 arrives at Stogumber with a morning train for Taunton on 15 August 1959.* Geoffrey F. Bannister

Bottom right: *The 14.20 through train to Paddington awaits departure from Minehead on Saturday 23 June 1962, double-headed by Standard Class 3MT No 82042 and WR Class 57xx pannier tank No 9635.* W. G. Sumner

Above: *Class 43xx 2-6-0 No 6372 leaves Wiveliscombe for Barnstaple Junction with an afternoon train from Taunton, having crossed No 7304 of the same class seen in the distance with a Barnstaple to Taunton train. The double track from Norton Fitzwarren ended at this point.* R. E. Toop

The Minehead and Barnstaple branches left the main line on the up side almost at the same point just west of Norton Fitzwarren. Both were single-track, but in the 1930s each branch was doubled as far as its first station, Bishops Lydeard and Milverton respectively, mainly to avoid down trains blocking the main line at Norton Fitzwarren while awaiting an up train off the branch. Beyond these points automatic token exchange was installed on both branches, so that crossing stations could be passed at up to 40mph.

At Tiverton Junction the Culm Valley branch train to Hemyock left from a loop platform on the down side. This line had been opened under a Light Railway Order in

1876 and required special lightweight coaches hauled or propelled usually by a Class 14xx tank engine, and by virtue of its milk traffic the branch remained open until 1975 (although closed to passengers in 1963). From a loop platform on the up side of Tiverton Junction another auto train plied to and from Tiverton, where it met the Exe Valley branch whose trains from Exeter to Dulverton themselves left the main line at Stoke Canon.

At Cowley Bridge junction up Southern Region trains from Ilfracombe, Padstow or Plymouth Friary joined the Western main line for the 1¼ miles to Exeter St Davids, and there used the middle island platform numbered 3 and 4. Shortly after Cowley Bridge is the entrance to the large Riverside goods yard on the up side. There are six platforms at Exeter St Davids. The principal down platform is No 1, the bay at the east end of which (Platform 2) was known as the Exe Valley bay from its use by the branch trains. Down nonstop Western trains use a through line between Platforms 1 and 3. The other island, numbered 5 and 6, was and is used by up Western Region trains, No 5 being the principal up platform.

Right: *Southern Region engines had regular workings over the Barnstaple to Taunton line. On 5 September 1953 Class T9 No 30710 calls at East Anstey with the 16.00 from Barnstaple Junction.* S. C. Nash

Centre right: *The down 'Torbay Express', 12.00 Paddington to Kingswear, begins the climb to Whiteball behind No 5023 Brecon Castle on Saturday 13 September 1952. On Saturdays in the summer the 'Torbay' ran nonstop from Paddington to Torquay.* R. H. G. Simpson

Bottom right: *The 13.35 from Paignton did not even call at Torquay, and conveyed passengers for Paddington only. Here the train descends Wellington bank with No 5028 Llantilio Castle of Newton Abbot shed at the front, also on 13 September 1952.* R. H. G. Simpson

Top: *The Culm Valley branch was kept busy by milk traffic from the dairy at Hemyock. On 23 July 1958 Class 14xx No 1449 nears Tiverton Junction with the 17.55 mixed train from Hemyock, consisting of five milk tanks and one passenger coach, and . . .*

Above: *. . . arrives in the branch platform on the down side at Tiverton Junction. The tanks will be attached to the 12.20 Penzance to Kensington milk train, due at Tiverton Junction at 19.00.* Both: R. C. Riley

Top right: *No 1451 has arrived at Hemyock with the 13.40 from Tiverton Junction on 26 June 1959. The coach is one of the gaslit former Barry Railway vehicles specially converted in the early 1950s for use on this branch.* D. J. Lane

Right: *On 24 February 1962 No 1462 propels four milk tanks from Hemyock to the rear of a stopping passenger train in the up platform at Tiverton Junction. The tanks will probably be detached at Wellington for the evening milk train to West Ealing. The Hemyock branch coach can be seen in the loop platform beyond the engine's chimney, and in the sidings on the extreme right is the gas tank wagon which supplied its lighting system.* T. W. Nicholls

Top: *Stoke Canon was the junction for the Exe Valley branch, and was another station enlarged in the 1930s to provide four running lines. On 30 June 1951 'Star' class No 4054* Princess Charlotte *calls at the down platform with a parcels train.* M. Maclee

Above: *Class T9 4-4-0 No 30717 passes the Great Western type home signal of Cowley Bridge junction on Saturday 22 August 1959, hauling the Plymouth and Padstow portions of the 16.30 Exeter Central to Waterloo.* S. C. Nash

Top: *On 16 July 1958 Class M7 No 30668 approaches Cowley Bridge junction with the Crediton to Exeter Central milk train.* R. C. Riley

Above: *The 11.39 Exeter Central to Plymouth, double-headed by 'Battle of Britain' No 34085* 501 Squadron *and Class N No 31844, meets No 34107* Blandford Forum *on an up Southern express for Waterloo on the Western Region main line near Cowley Bridge junction on Saturday 16 July 1960. The tracks on the far right are goods lines leading to Riverside yard.* R. C. Riley

Above: *The 14-coach 07.40 St Austell to Wolverhampton approaches Cowley Bridge Junction on 6 July 1957, double-headed by 'Hall' class No 4970* Sketty Hall *and 'Modified Hall' No 7901* Dodington Hall. *No 7901, shedded at Bristol (Bath Road), was carrying the train reporting number 670; No 4970, the pilot, was allocated to Taunton shed and may well have been detached there after assisting on the climb to Whiteball.* R. C. Riley

Below: *On 20 July 1956 the 17.36 Crediton to Exeter Central milk train, hauled by Class M7 No 30676, has arrived in Platform 3 at Exeter St Davids and two milk tanks are detached by the east end station pilot, Class 2251 0-6-0 No 2230. They will be placed in a siding to be picked up by the train engine (Class 47xx No 4701) of the 12.20 Penzance to Kensington milk and added to the front of its train.* R. C. Riley

Above: 'Castle' class No 5065 Newport Castle, on the 13.15 Plymouth to Liverpool, is held in Platform 5 at Exeter St Davids for the departure from Platform 4 of No 34079 141 Squadron with a late-running portion of the down 'Atlantic Coast Express'. Photographed in February 1962. B. R. Oliver

Below: A Sunday Penzance to Paddington express passes Exeter West box and enters Platform 5 at St Davids on 1 September 1957. The engine is an Old Oak Common 'Castle', No 5052 Earl of Radnor. The Southern line to Exeter Central can be seen curving round to the left, and on the right are the lines leading to Platform 6 and the engine shed and carriage sidings. J. C. Way

Summer Saturdays

Every Saturday in the holiday season the same series of expresses left Paddington for Paignton or Penzance, Minehead, Newquay or St Ives. Most had long nonstop runs, even though some were timed positively slowly. In the middle of the morning they left in groups, centred on the regular departure times at 09.30, 10.30 and 11.00; starting at five minute intervals, the group would be nearer 10 minutes apart beyond Reading, where block sections were longer, but if you were standing to leeward of the trains, by the time the last traces of smoke had cleared it was never long before the signals were being pulled off again.

The down 'Limited' did not slip a portion at Westbury on a summer Saturday. Instead the main restaurant car train ran to St Ives, with four coaches at the rear for Penzance, and the first passenger stop was at Truro. The 10.35 Paddington was the main Penzance train, with a rear portion for Falmouth. Both trains were regularly 14 coaches long.

In the up direction an immense group of trains from Devon and Cornwall to Paddington followed one another through Taunton at lunchtime, and all afternoon the Marlborough Downs and the woods above Beenham echoed to the distant clack of wheels on rails. The following is a list of these trains as they passed Savernake. The times are for 1956, though the details varied little over the years.

Afternoon Up Traffic through Savernake (1956)

Scheduled to pass Savernake (Low Level) at	Train from	Reporting number	Last passenger stop	Remarks
14.13	11.30 Torquay	525	Torquay	
14.22	08.15 Perranporth	610	Par	
14.32	08.35 Falmouth	615	Liskeard	
14.42	11.20 Kingswear	520	Torquay	'Torbay Express'
14.55	11.15 Plymouth 10.55 Kingsbridge	620	Newton Abbot	
15.06	12.18 Newton Abbot	529	Exeter	
15.20	09.20 St Ives	630	Plymouth	
15.35	10.00 Newquay	638	St Columb Road	
15.45	08.20 Penzance	625	Taunton and Reading	
15.59	10.00 Penzance	635	Plymouth	'Cornish Riviera Limited'

On a summer Saturday, Newbury was served by two West of England expresses in each direction. The 07.25 Ealing Broadway to Penzance picked up passengers at Slough, Maidenhead, Twyford and Reading, then called at Newbury and Frome, but not Westbury. Later in the day the 12.05 Paddington to Plymouth stopped at Newbury to pick up only, and then ran nonstop to Taunton. In the up direction the two stops on a Saturday evening gave an excellent service for anyone returning from a holiday in the west. The 13.55 Torquay to Paddington stopped only at Newbury in its whole journey, and the 11.50 Penzance (the 'Royal Duchy'), which called every evening in the summer, on Saturdays ran nonstop from Plymouth to Newbury (excluding the

Right: *On a summer Saturday the main Penzance portion of the 'Cornish Riviera Express' was conveyed by the following 10.35 from Paddington, which also had through coaches to Falmouth and made its first passenger stop at Plymouth. Both were regular 14-coach trains. Burlescombe distant signal is off as the 10.35 clears Whiteball summit on 27 July 1957, headed by No 6025* King Henry III.
Kenneth Leech

Below: *A train on which a Class 47xx 2-8-0 might be seen on a busy Saturday was the 12.05 Paddington to Plymouth. No 4700 passes Ranelagh Bridge at the head of 11 coaches on 6 August 1960.* R. C. Riley

working stop at Newton Abbot to detach a pilot engine). Slough was served in the late evening by the 16.15 Paignton to Paddington, nonstop from Torquay.

Westbury had a through train to Minehead on a Saturday morning, calling only at Taunton; this was the 09.35 Paddington, which connected with a Saturday-only semi-fast from Reading to Weymouth (via Devizes). Frome had its through Saturday train to Penzance shortly before 10.00 but no corresponding up train.

Besides the usual 'Kings' and 'Castles', the summer Saturday expresses were hauled by any of the smaller Great Western 4-6-0s, the 'Halls', 'Counties' and 'Granges', and in the early 1950s by the last remaining members of the 'Star' and 'Saint' classes. The 'Cornish Riviera Limited' was the only invariable 'King' working in the down direction; of the up trains, those from Perranporth and St Ives, the principal Newquay train and the 'Limited' usually, though not always, had 'Kings'. The harder turns were marked out for at least a 'Castle', but by the end of July a 'Hall', usually 'Modified' if available, could be seen on such trains as the 09.30 Paddington to Newquay and 11.00 to Penzance, or even a 'Grange' on the 10.20 Paddington to Kingswear. Old Oak Common not infrequently provided a Class 47xx 2-8-0, designed for fast freights, to work a summer Saturday passenger express, although they were not supposed to exceed 60mph. In the early 1950s these engines appeared on various trains, even the down 'Torbay Express', but later were largely confined to the 12.05 Paddington to Plymouth and 13.25 Paddington to Kingswear; instead of the latter a '47xx' frequently hauled the following down 'Royal Duchy' during the 1958 season. '47xx' workings in the up direction were more occasional, but once in 1958 Laira shed sent its only member of the class to Paddington on the 10.00 train from Newquay. In 1959 and 1960 Standard Class 9F 2-10-0 freight engines,

recently allocated in large numbers to the Western Region, were used on some of the Saturday trains and for the most part replaced the '47xx' class. Even at periods of peak demand on the motive power department, Class 43xx 2-6-0s and '28xx' 2-8-0s were not turned out to work expresses between Paddington and the West.

The majority of the engines of the Saturday expresses came from Old Oak Common, Newton Abbot or Laira sheds, but engines from other parts of the Western Region were not uncommon. For the morning rush of down trains, the Old Oak Common allocation was regularly supplemented by the sheds at Southall, Reading and Didcot; Southall usually provided the engine for one of the first two trains of the day, the 06.55 Paddington to Penzance or 07.00 to Kingswear; Reading shed sent engines up to Paddington on local trains, and for some years one (usually a 'Hall') was scheduled to run light all the way to Ranelagh Bridge, turn there and work the 07.40 Paddington to Paignton; Didcot engines came up on early morning trains of empty coaches, and the 07.10 Didcot to Paddington passenger, due at 08.35, was usually double-headed, to provide an extra engine for a morning departure.

The engines of the West of England extras worked through at least between Paddington and Newton Abbot, the Torquay branch or Plymouth. The only exceptions

Right: The 09.35 (SO) Paddington to Minehead was normally worked by a Didcot 'Hall' which had arrived in London during the early hours with one of the empty trains from Didcot. On 6 August 1955 the 09.35 is seen near Cole behind No 6952 Kimberley Hall; it was too long a train for the Minehead branch and so on arrival at Taunton the main line engine would remove the front three or four coaches to bring the load within a maximum of nine coaches. Kenneth Leech

Left: *A view of the down Saturday 'Royal Duchy' in the summer of 1958, departing from Platform 1 at Exeter St Davids on 19 July. The train engine is No 4701 which will work as far as Plymouth North Road (like the 'Kings', the 47xx class was not permitted to cross Saltash bridge). Piloting the 2-8-0 is No 6839* Hewell Grange, *of Oxley shed near Wolverhampton, which has an empty reporting number frame attached to the front of the smokebox; according to the regular Saturday working the 'Grange' would have reached Taunton on a Wolverhampton to Minehead and Ilfracombe train and then piloted the 'Royal Duchy' through to Plymouth.* R. C. Riley

were the through Minehead trains, whose engines worked as far as Taunton, where a smaller engine, usually a tank, took over part of the train and hauled it on the branch. If the train was not conveying an Ilfracombe portion, coaches were detached from the front at Taunton to bring the Minehead load within a maximum of nine coaches. Unlike in the 1930s, when some Paddington to Minehead trains changed engines on the goods line at Taunton, in the 1950s all made passenger stops at the station.

The Saturday trains were heavily loaded. On a peak day at the end of July or in August, as many as half the morning departures from Paddington to the West of England might be 14-coach trains, several of them in the hands of two-cylinder 'Halls' or 'Modified Halls'. One train invariably loaded to 15 coaches, the 10.00 Newquay to Paddington (except on the occasion already noted when it was hauled by a '47xx' 2-8-0).

The stock of these trains was very mixed, in age, design and at times livery, and might include ex-Great Western coaches up to 50 years old as well as vehicles from other Regions. Business sets of various kinds made their way along the Taunton main line en route for the west on summer Saturdays. After the reintroduction of chocolate and cream in 1956, the coaches of the 'Bristolian' (which did not run on Saturdays) were included in the 07.00 Paddington to Kingswear, and the next year in the 08.50

Paddington to Paignton. The stock of the 'Inter-City', a Monday to Friday express between Paddington, Birmingham and Wolverhampton, formed the main portion of the 10.35 to Penzance and Falmouth, returning to Paddington on the Sunday. Commuter sets were also used; in the summer of 1957, for instance, the coaches of three evening trains from Paddington, two to Henley and one to Didcot, were worked up empty on Saturday mornings to form trains to Paignton or Kingswear. The dining car for the 10.20 Paddington to Kingswear was added (unstaffed) to the stock of the 17.15 Paddington to Henley on a Friday evening. The 18.15 Paddington included some non-corridor coaches; these were separated at Henley and the corridor coaches sent up to form the 10.40 Paddington to Paignton, a light train running on a few peak Saturdays only. In that year three empty trains in all came up from Didcot early on a Saturday; the second generally provided the engine for the 09.35 Paddington to Minehead, which would go down to Taunton with 'No 2' still chalked on the smokebox door.

Most of the principal expresses to Paddington on Saturdays had restaurant cars, and they even worked throughout from Perranporth, Newquay and St Ives. On a Friday morning in summer, after the departure of the 'Inter-City' at 09.00, Platform 4 at Paddington was set aside for the provisioning of dining cars for the Saturday extras. Two trains were loaded in succession, each being at the platform for about an hour and a half. The first returned to Old Oak Common and consisted of the diners for the next day's down trains; the second departed at 12.05, the main part of the train destined for Newquay, and provided dining cars for four or five of the up expresses from Devon and Cornwall.

Most Paddington to West of England expresses carried a train reporting number every weekday, but on a summer Saturday practically all expresses did so, including some Weymouth trains which were

unnumbered for the rest of the week. It was to cope with the confusion on summer Saturdays, particularly west of Taunton, that reporting numbers were first introduced in 1934. All consisted of three figures, and the number of a train depended on its place of origin. Trains from London (up to and including summer 1958) were numbered in the 100s; those starting in the Exeter division began with five and those from Plymouth or Cornwall with six. The numbers of most of the regular Saturday up trains ended in zero or five, the intervening numbers having been intended for reliefs. When engine sheds ran out of numbers, they were either chalked on the front of the engine, usually remaining there for several days, or carried on a small placard, apparently known as a ticket, beneath the chimney.

There were no Saturday extras from Paddington to Weymouth Town, Waterloo being the principal station for Weymouth, but the down Jersey boat train ran in two portions. Instead of the various stops of the midweek train, the advance relief was advertised nonstop to Weymouth Quay, and the main train as calling only at Reading to take up passengers; in practice, however, both stopped to change crews at Heywood Road junction, and made further stops on the Weymouth line for banking assistance and engine changing. For most of the 1950s they left Paddington at 08.20 and 08.30, and were separated as far as Castle Cary by the 08.25 to Penzance and Perranporth. Coming back, the extra summer boat sailings were on Saturday nights, and at peak weekends

Above: *Every Friday in the summer season a train of empty restaurant cars, but carrying express passenger headlamps, left Paddington for the West of England at 12.05. The restaurant cars were taken to Plymouth and Newquay, and in some years Newton Abbot, to be formed in the Saturday holiday expresses for London. On 3 September 1954 'Modified Hall' No 6978* Haroldstone Hall *had charge of the train and is seen passing Exeter Middle Box and Red Cow level crossing and running into Platform 1 at St Davids, where a stop was scheduled for the gassing of the restaurant cars. The front coach is a brake third which provided extra accommodation for the restaurant crews.* J. N. Faulkner

Above right: *On a summer Saturday in the 1950s two trains for returning holidaymakers started at Torquay in mid-morning and ran nonstop to Paddington. On 11 August 1956 No 6926* Holkham Hall *makes the steady ascent towards Brewham signalbox, east of Castle Cary, with the 10.35 from Torquay.* Kenneth Leech

Right: *The 11.30 Torquay nears Whiteball summit and the end of 20 miles almost continuous climbing from Exeter. The date is 28 July 1956 and the engine No 4996* Eden Hall. *In the middle of a July Saturday trains would be passing Whiteball every six minutes in each direction.* Kenneth Leech

two boat trains left Weymouth Quay for Paddington early on Sunday morning. But from 1955 there was an additional train from Weymouth Town to Paddington on summer Saturdays, which continued to leave Weymouth

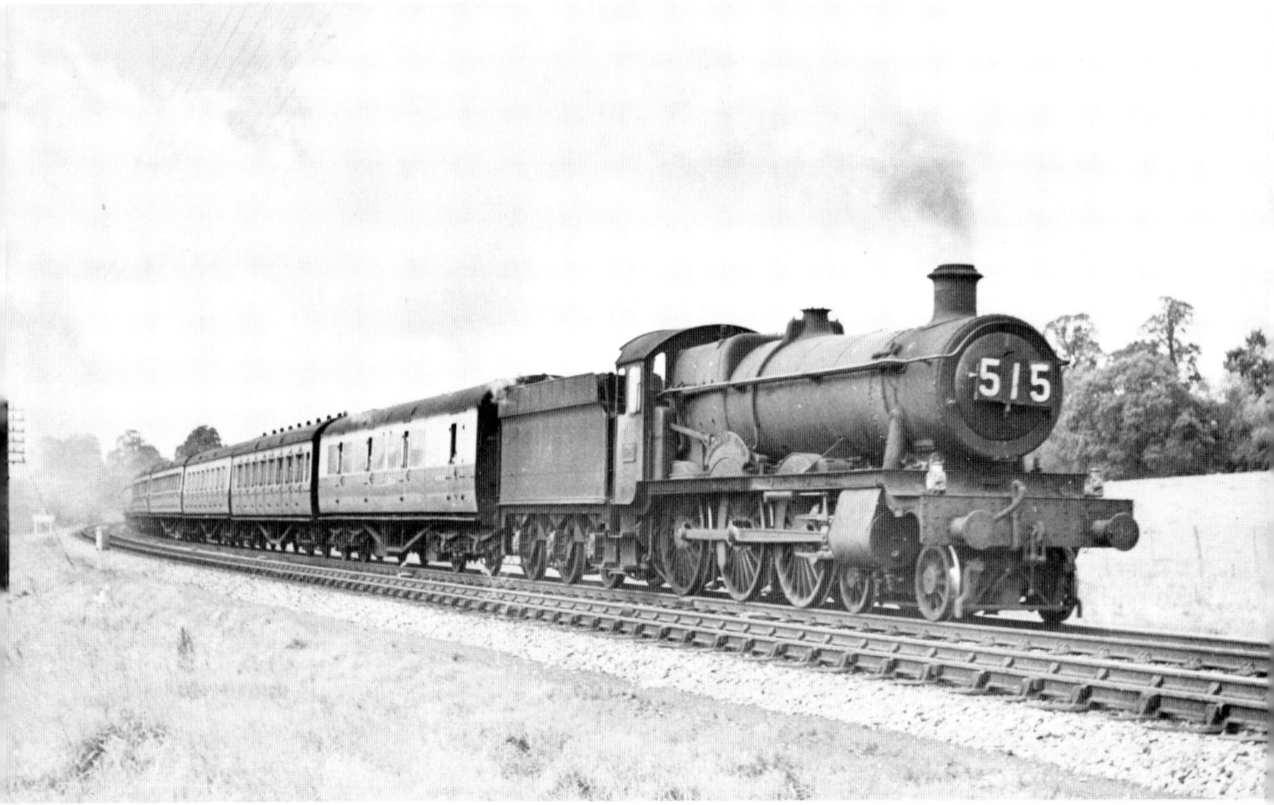
515

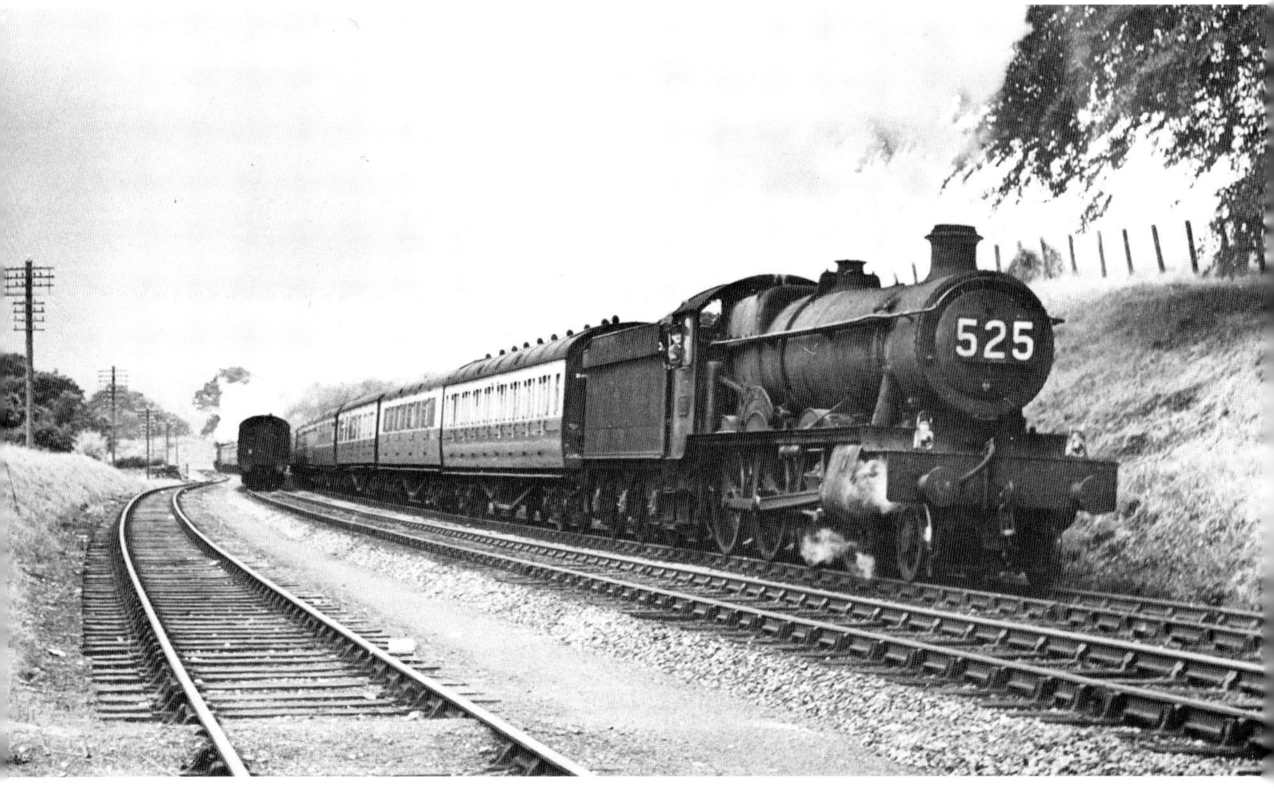
525

at 11.12 after its daily counterpart had been withdrawn. This train, worked throughout by a Westbury 'Hall', was scheduled to reach Castle Cary just after the passing of the nonstop 10.35 Torquay to Paddington, and continue east in the long gap before the group of expresses listed on page 114.

The trains in this group were not tightly timed from Taunton to Paddington; in particular the first, the 11.30 from Torquay, with a three-hour allowance from Taunton, was often 10 or 15 minutes ahead of time by Reading. But however well they appeared to be running at first, sooner or later in the afternoon there was usually a hiatus. Often it was the 11.15 Plymouth or the 12.18 Newton Abbot which was held up somewhere. When Paddington's arrival indicator showed several 99s in the minutes late column — it had only two digits — it was usually assumed that the congested tracks west of Taunton were responsible for the delay. In fact a surprising amount of time was lost, in both directions, between Reading and Taunton. The line was almost entirely double-track with several conflicting flows of traffic; although there were many more block sections than there are now, local traffic was, at least in parts, relatively intensive, and in the 90 miles from Newbury to Taunton there were virtually no overtaking points except at Westbury and Frome. Expresses tended to run in batches; a local train might be held back for two

or three late-running expresses, but after that most signalmen would allow the local to make a dash for it. A typical delay happened one Saturday in August 1955, when the 12.18 Newton Abbot to Paddington stopped for water at Castle Cary and held up several following expresses; because of adverse signals the train had been travelling too slowly to take water at Creech troughs.

The first conflicting traffic flow was between Oxford Road junction and Southcote junction, Reading, a stretch of line used by cross-country trains for the Southern Region. There were many extra trains to and from Bournemouth and, more particularly, Portsmouth, mostly coming from Birmingham or Wolverhampton. There were turns for four Southern engines, usually 'King Arthurs', to Oxford and back, instead of the regular two, and '43xx' 2-6-0s sometimes worked through to Basingstoke. A number of the southbound extras came down overnight; up trains reached Southcote junction in a steady stream from Basingstoke, the last cross-country extra in the later 1950s, from Portsmouth to Sheffield, not passing Reading West until after 18.30. The following table shows how a series of trains from the Midlands to Portsmouth had to be inserted among the mid-morning departures from Paddington. The times are those for 1957: main line trains were timed at Reading General, cross-country trains at Reading West, and an express would take $1\frac{1}{2}$ to 2 minutes between the two stations.

West of England and Midlands-Portsmouth trains through Reading (1957)

Reading General Pass or depart	Reading West Pass or stop	
10.10		09.30 Paddington-Newquay
10.15		09.35 Paddington-Minehead
10.22		09.40 Paddington-Paignton
	10.35	07.48 Wolverhampton-Portsmouth
10.38		10.38 Reading-Newbury diesel
10.45	10.48/10.49*	10.45 Reading-Basingstoke
	10.59	08.40 Birmingham (Moor Street)-Portsmouth
11.01		10.20 Paddington-Kingswear
11.11		10.30 Paddington-St Ives, Penzance
11.16		10.35 Paddington-Penzance, Falmouth
11.21		10.40 Paddington-Paignton
	11.27	09.05 Birmingham (Snow Hill)-Portsmouth
	11.32	08.40 Wolverhampton-Portsmouth
11.41		11.00 Paddington-Penzance, Kingsbridge
11.46		11.05 Paddington-Penzance
	11.49	09.28 Birmingham (Snow Hill)-Portsmouth
11.51		11.51 Reading-Hungerford

* Arrival and departure times

The 09.28 from Birmingham was scheduled to stop at Oxford Road junction from 11.42 to 11.48, while the 11.00 and 11.05 Paddington went by on the main line. In addition to the trains listed, between 10.03 and 11.59 Southcote junction signalbox was booked to receive seven trains from the Southern Region, whose paths there conflicted with those of the down West of England expresses; five of these were cross-country extras from

Bournemouth or Portsmouth to Newcastle, Birkenhead, Birmingham or Wolverhampton.

From 1953 to 1961 the Didcot, Newbury & Southampton line was used once a year, on the Saturday after August bank holiday, for a relief train from Portsmouth Harbour to Birmingham or Wolverhampton, which generally changed from a Southern to a Western Region engine at Newbury. In 1957 this train was

Above: *'Modified Hall' No 6959* Peatling Hall *recovers from a signal check at the approach to Hungerford on Saturday 12 July 1958 with the 12-coach 08.50 Paddington to Paignton (first stop Exeter). No 6959 had been catching up with the train in front, the 08.30 Paddington to Weymouth Quay with No 5093* Upton Castle *on 13 coaches, which had also been checked at Hungerford; the block section ahead to Bedwyn was nearly five miles long on a steady uphill gradient. The front coaches of the 08.50 are chocolate-and-cream and may have been the Monday to Friday 'Bristolian' set.* R. C. Riley

scheduled to wait 10 minutes at Enborne junction, where its route joined the Berks & Hants main line, for the 11.12 Weymouth to Paddington to pass, and then follow the Weymouth train into Newbury. There it changed engines and ran as far as Leamington Spa without a booked passenger stop.

Many additional trains between Portsmouth and Bristol or Cardiff, and some from Bournemouth, passed through Westbury on a summer Saturday, all stopping at the station, but did not really conflict with the West of England traffic, the bulk of which used the avoiding line. There were, however, a number of extra trains for the Weymouth line, mostly to and from Birmingham, some of which passed nonstop through Westbury, and which shared the line with the West of England expresses between Fairwood junction and Castle Cary. There was

also a Saturday train from Wolverhampton to Paignton via Oxford, Swindon and Westbury, and a corresponding up train which in most years started from Torquay at 10.00 and ran to Wolverhampton or Birmingham (Moor Street); neither train stopped at Westbury. The 09.35 Paddington to Minehead made its first stop at Westbury and was overtaken by the 09.40 Paddington to Paignton on the avoiding line. In the same manner an afternoon Kingswear to Paddington train with a number of stops was overtaken by one from Paignton which was nonstop from Torquay to Paddington. An hour or so later an up train from Weymouth was divided at Westbury. This was the 16.05 Weymouth Quay to Cardiff and Birmingham, which connected with the day sailing from the Channel Islands, and which included at the front a portion from Weymouth Town to Cardiff. The Birmingham coaches were detached at Westbury and made up a separate train from there onwards.

The following table shows how the principal group of Saturday trains to Weymouth had to be fitted in at Fairwood junction to the procession of expresses from Paddington, some of which featured in the Reading table. Trains which stopped at Frome could be overtaken, but there was no overtaking point for nearly 13 miles from Blatchbridge junction to Castle Cary. The times are for 1955, and those trains which had no scheduled passing time for Fairwood junction would be expected to pass there in three or four minutes from Westbury.

Saturday traffic at Fairwood junction (1955)

Westbury Depart or pass	Fairwood junction pass	Castle Cary pass or stop	Train	Intermediate stops
09.27		10.03/10.05	09.27 Westbury-Weymouth	Frome, Witham, Bruton
	09.38	10.11	07.25 Ealing Broadway-Penzance	Frome
09.47		—	09.47 Westbury-Bristol via Wells	Frome, Witham
09.57*		10.27	09.10 Bristol-Weymouth	Frome
	10.13	10.34	08.10 Paddington-Paignton	
	10.24	10.44	08.20 Paddington-Weymouth Quay	
	10.30	10.51	08.25 Paddington, Penzance, Perranporth	
	10.39	11.01	08.30 Paddington-Weymouth Quay	
	10.46	11.08	08.50 Paddington-Paignton	
10.50	10.54	11.19/11.21	08.30 Weston-super-Mare- Weymouth	
11.03½*	11.06	11.27	07.50 Birmingham (Snow Hill)- Weymouth Town	
	11.14	11.33	09.30 Paddington-Newquay	
11.18*	11.21	11.41	08.00 Birmingham (Snow Hill)- Weymouth Town and Quay	
	11.32	11.51	09.40 Paddington-Paignton	
11.38	11.41	12.01	09.35 Paddington-Minehead	
11.44	11.47½	12.15/12.17	09.34 Reading-Weymouth	Frome

* nonstop through Westbury

There were further conflicting movements at Castle Cary, four up Weymouth trains being scheduled to join the main line there between 10.13 and 11.37. One of these was for Paddington and three for Birmingham or Wolverhampton.

The main group of up West of England expresses (listed on page 114) was scheduled (in 1955) to pass Castle Cary between 13.18 and 15.10. During these two hours only two other up trains were booked, both from Weymouth to Bristol. The first omitted its weekday Frome stop and ran fast from Yeovil to Westbury; the second called at Castle Cary and Frome, where the up 'Cornish Riviera Limited' was scheduled to overtake on the avoiding line. During the same period four down trains from the Westbury line conflicted with the up expresses at Fairwood junction, and three of the four had to cross the up main line twice more to call at Frome.

Over the sections of main line on which stopping trains were normally run, there was nowhere an express could overtake (unless the local train was shunted) between Reading General and Newbury, Newbury and Patney & Chirton, or Castle Cary and Athelney. The first down long-distance stopping train from Reading, the 08.10 to Bristol, was retimed to depart earlier on a Saturday in the summer, but was put into the bay platform at Newbury for 20 minutes to allow the 07.40 Paddington to Paignton and 07.25 Ealing Broadway to Penzance (which called at the down main platform) to overtake; meanwhile the 07.40 Didcot to Southampton, which normally occupied the down bay, had to use the loading dock. Other stopping trains in the area had their timings altered on a Saturday, sometimes with extended waits at Newbury. In the afternoon some up local trains were forced to run express to Reading to keep out of the way; the twin diesel unit made two consecutive eastbound journeys from Newbury either nonstop or calling at Thatcham only. Further west the morning Bristol to Reading stopping train via Devizes was altered to run earlier, and booked to wait in the loop at Patney for an express from Plymouth.

Between Castle Cary and Taunton the times of stopping trains were also changed to suit the flow of expresses. The morning down train, leaving Castle Cary at 10.18, was scheduled to be shunted at Somerton for 26 minutes while the 08.10 Paddington to Paignton and 08.25 to Penzance went by, and thenceforth advertised times differed from working times in the manner already described. Two afternoon trains from Taunton to Yeovil, which set out via the Durston line, had scheduled waits of the order of ten minutes at Athelney for up expresses to pass. But the lunchtime trains from Yeovil to Taunton and vice versa were not allowed on to the main line at all, and, having reached Langport West, the train went back to Yeovil, passengers for Taunton having to continue by bus. In later years a pathway was found for these trains between Athelney and Taunton; but the up train's departure from Taunton at 12.35 was just in front of the main group of Paddington expresses (see page 114), and so it was hustled to Langport West without a stop, where it waited half-an-hour before proceeding to Yeovil.

A few hours at Reading General in 1959

On 8 August 1959, in addition to the mass of Saturdays-only trains, up to 16.00 eight reliefs had passed through Reading, not counting a number of other trains which were unadvertised but appeared in the working timetable either as regular Saturday services or to run only when required. Of the eight, three ran to or from the West of England using the Berks & Hants route via Newbury. The 07.15 Paignton to Paddington relief hauled by No 1012 *County of Denbigh* consisted mainly of saloon excursion stock, while following it up the main line from Reading was a train from Abertillery, South Wales, which included a number of chocolate and cream coaches with 'Paddington Torquay Paignton and Dartmouth' roofboards. The 07.25 Plymouth and 09.05 Minehead to Paddington, normally combined at Taunton, ran as separate trains though of only eight and six coaches respectively; the other West of England relief left Paddington at 06.55 for Paignton.

In 1959 the first of the 'Warship' class diesel-hydraulic locomotives were in use, notably on the West of England line, both the D8xx and the less successful D6xx series. On 8 August D808 *Centaur* took the 10.35 Paddington to Penzance and Falmouth through Reading, while the preceding 'Cornish Riviera Express' was in the hands of the traditional 'King', and further west these two locomotives no doubt double-headed the 10.35 between Newton Abbot and Plymouth. Half an hour later the 11.00 and 11.05 Paddington to Penzance passed Reading with No 6003 *King George IV* followed by No D601 *Ark Royal*. On that Saturday no less than three Class 9F 2-10-0s were on passenger turns to or from the west. The 13-coach up 'Mayflower' from Plymouth stopped at Reading 42 minutes late (the slip coach was no longer conveyed in 1959 — but had not operated on summer Saturdays anyway) behind No 92206; and No 92230 also had 13 crowded coaches on the 13.25 Paddington to Kingswear. No 92221 was 17 minutes late on the 12.05 Paddington to Plymouth, having lost its path through Reading to a train from Margate to Wolverhampton. The only Class 47xx 2-8-0 seen on passenger work that day came through 11 minutes early on the 13.50 Bristol to Paddington, having travelled at just over a mile a minute from its last stop at Swindon, assuming it did not leave there before time; at that moment, 15.39, as many as six up West of England expresses in the group led by the 11.30 Torquay were overdue, and soon the Torquay train came past, not untypically a little over three-quarters of an hour late. The 07.40 Paddington to Paignton, whose engine was booked to leave Reading for London at 05.55 running light, was hauled by one of Reading shed's

Left: Sometimes the 'Britannia' Pacifics were to be seen on the West of England main line. On 2 July 1955 No 70017 Arrow, *then allocated to Old Oak Common, passes Castle Cary 35 minutes late at 15.02 with the Saturday 09.20 St Ives to Paddington. The passengers on the up platform are awaiting the 15.01 to Bristol, a Weymouth train which has no doubt been delayed by expresses from the West, while at the down platform the 14.58 auto train to Taunton is also overdue.* R. C. Riley

'Castles', No 5018 *St Mawes Castle*, and, as scheduled, passed through the down main platform while the 07.25 Ealing Broadway to Penzance waited on the down relief line. The 08.00 Kingswear to Paddington, nonstop between Dawlish and Reading, was pulled by No 6813 *Eastbury Grange* of Newton Abbot shed.

From 07.40 to 10.40 six trains, each formed of 10 coaches, left Paddington for the Kingswear branch, all but one terminating at Paignton. The 08.10, 08.50 and 09.40 were seriously overcrowded, the worst being the 08.50 which in previous years had consisted of up to 14 coaches (even 15 on one occasion in 1957). The policy in 1959 was to limit these trains to a load that could be managed by a single engine on the climb out of Torquay in the up direction, so as to reduce light engine working in that area. The 08.10 and 10.15 had the numbers '2' and '4' respectively pasted in the windows of the end coaches, showing that they were part of the series of empty trains that had been worked up to Paddington from Didcot and Henley that morning. Many departures for other parts of the West of England loaded to 13 or 14 coaches as usual, notably the 09.35 Paddington to Minehead, 13 coaches behind No 6908 *Downham Hall*, which had fallen behind the 09.30 Newquay train to the extent of 16 minutes by Reading and was being hard pressed by the lightly loaded 09.40. The front four coaches of the 09.35 were labelled for Taunton and would be detached there, so as to bring the train within the capacity of the Minehead branch engine.

The late running of trains on that Saturday created operating problems on several occasions. At 15.00 the 11.12 Weymouth to Paddington, running 19 minutes late, and the 11.45 from Cheltenham Spa, 41 minutes late, were approaching Reading on their separate routes. The Weymouth train called at the up main platform as usual while the Cheltenham train was diverted to the up relief (Platform 9). They started simultaneously, but the Cheltenham train was stopped again to allow the other to get ahead, before being switched to the main line behind it. Two of Gloucester's 'Castles' double-headed the 14-coach 11.45 Cheltenham, and while it was in the Reading area two more 'Castles' from the same shed passed successively in the down direction on the two portions of the 14.15 Paddington to Cheltenham.

A major traffic flow encountered by West of England trains east of Reading was that to and from South Wales. Between 09.16 and 12.56 on 8 August 1959 as many as 12 trains from this area passed through Reading in the up direction alone, nine of them without stopping. Three of these were Saturday through trains from the Welsh valleys, introduced the previous summer, originating respectively at Blaina, Abertillery and Ebbw Vale and all running nonstop from Newport to Paddington. At 09.23 the 'King'-hauled 07.00 Weston-super-Mare to Paddington passed Reading on the up through line, overtaking two more London expresses which followed in succession. Standing in Platform 5 (up main) at the time was the 07.15 from Trowbridge, while in Platform 9 was the 03.35 Fishguard Harbour, the first of four trains connecting with overnight steamers from Rosslare or Cork. The 03.35 was timed very slowly, being allowed 35 minutes to run on the relief line from Didcot to Reading (17 miles), and on this occasion stood in the platform at Reading for 12 minutes.

Another flow of traffic through Reading, none of which survived in the late 1970s, was between the Midlands and the Kent coast via Guildford and Redhill. From one train in each direction on weekdays the service expanded to seven trains passing Reading between 12.08 and 13.34 on that 1959 Saturday (and two more later in the afternoon). It was the end of the Birmingham holiday fortnight and northbound trains were particularly crowded. The Saturday extras either changed engines outside Reading South station or were worked by Western Region engines to or from Redhill, but the regular train in each direction changed engines in the platform at Reading General. The first two trains from Margate, the 08.50 and 09.02 departures, passed nonstop through Reading's down main platform behind Class 43xx 2-6-0s. These were followed by a relief from Margate whose Western Region engine, No 5911 *Preston Hall*, en route from Reading shed had been held in Platform 5 for the 09.05 Minehead to pass, then had to wait for the Class 9F on the 12.05 Paddington before taking the spur to the Southern line, and reappeared with its train after only 10 minutes. While the train, consisting of Southern Region stock with passengers standing in all the corridors, was being dealt with in Platform 4, No 7917 *North Aston Hall* on the 12.30 Paddington to Weymouth was waiting at signals outside and arrived six minutes late. As soon as the Weymouth train had left, its place was taken by Class N No 31863 of Redhill shed with the main train from Kent, the 08.56 Ramsgate to Birkenhead. Meanwhile 'Castle' No 5061 *Earl of Birkenhead* had brought the 13-coach 07.35 from Birkenhead, formed for Ramsgate, Deal and Margate, into the up main platform. This train spent 20 minutes changing engines to Standard 4MT No 76057, and probably contributed to the lateness of the up 'Mayflower' which followed it into the platform.

List of Signalboxes in 1951-2

KEY

- • Station with signalbox(es)
- o Station with no signalbox
- x Signalbox - no station

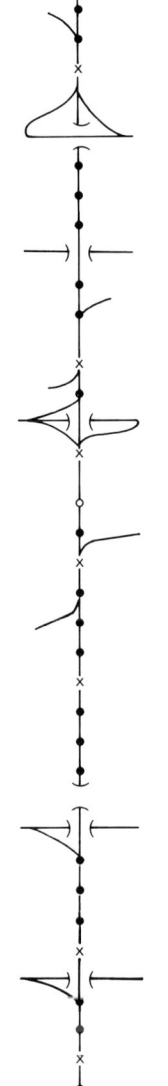

Waterloo
Vauxhall
Loco Junction

Queen's Road

West London Junction

Clapham Junction A
Earlsfield

Wimbledon A,B,C

Raynes Park

Malden

Berrylands
Surbiton
Hampton Court Junction

Esher East,West
Hersham
Walton
Oatlands
Weybridge

Byfleet Junction
West Weybridge
West Byfleet
Woking

Brookwood

Sturt Lane Junction

Farnborough
Fleet

Winchfield
Hook
Basingstoke A,B
Worting Junction

Oakley
Overton
Whitchurch North

Hurstbourne
Andover Junction East,
                West
Red Post Junction
Grateley

Amesbury Junction
 (later Allington)
Idmiston Halt
Porton
Salisbury Tunnel Junction
Salisbury East,West
Wilton South
Dinton
Chilmark Siding
Tisbury
Semley
Gillingham

Templecombe
Milborne Port
Sherborne
Wyke

Yeovil Junction A,B
Sutton Bingham
Hardington
Crewkerne
Hewish
Chard Junction
Broom
Axminster

Seaton Junction
Honiton Incline
Honiton
Sidmouth Junction
Whimple
Broad Clyst
Pinhoe
Exmouth Junction
St James Park Halt
Exeter Central A,B
Exeter St Davids

Paddington   Arrival, Departure
Westbourne Bridge

Subway Junction
Westbourne Park
Portobello Junction
Ladbroke Grove

Old Oak Common East
Old Oak Common West

Friars Junction

Acton East, Middle, West
Ealing Broadway
Longfield Avenue
West Ealing
Hanwell & Elthorne
Southall Junction East, West
          Station East, West

Hayes
Dawley
West Drayton East, West

Iver
Langley
Dolphin Junction
Slough East, Middle
Slough West
Farnham Road
Burnham
Taplow
Maidenhead East, Middle, West
Waltham Siding
Shottesbrook
Ruscombe
Twyford East, West

Woodley Bridge
Sonning

Kennet Bridge
Reading Main Line East, West
Oxford Road Junction
Reading West
Southcote Junction
Calcot
Theale
Ufton Crossing
Aldermaston
Midgham
Colthrop Siding
Thatcham Station, West
Bulls Lock
Newbury Racecourse
Newbury East Junction,
          Middle, West
Enborne Junction
Hamstead Crossing
Kintbury
Hungerford
Bedwyn
Grafton East Junction

Wolfhall Junction
Savernake low level
          East, West
Wootton Rivers Halt
Pewsey
Manningford Halt
Woodborough
Patney & Chirton
Crookwood
Lavington
Edington & Bratton
Heywood Road Junction

Westbury North, Middle, South

Fairwood Junction
Clink Road Junction

Frome North, South
Blatchbridge Junction
Woodlands
Witham
Brewham
Bruton

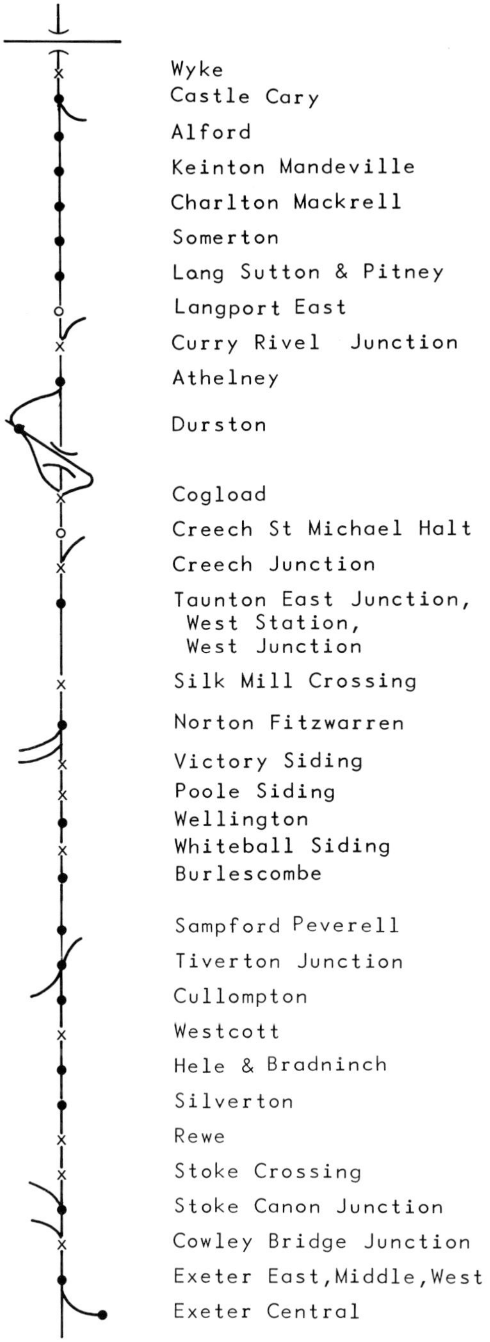

Wyke

Castle Cary

Alford

Keinton Mandeville

Charlton Mackrell

Somerton

Lang Sutton & Pitney

Langport East

Curry Rivel   Junction

Athelney

Durston

Cogload

Creech St Michael Halt

Creech Junction

Taunton East Junction,
 West Station,
 West Junction

Silk Mill Crossing

Norton Fitzwarren

Victory Siding
Poole Siding
Wellington
Whiteball Siding
Burlescombe

Sampford Peverell

Tiverton Junction

Cullompton

Westcott

Hele & Bradninch

Silverton

Rewe

Stoke Crossing

Stoke Canon Junction

Cowley Bridge Junction

Exeter East, Middle, West

Exeter Central